A BASIC Programmer's Guide to Pascal

More than a million people have learned to program, use, and enjoy micro-computers with Wiley paperback guides. Look for them all at your favorite bookshop or computer store:

ANS COBOL, 2nd Ed., Ashley
Apple™ BASIC: Data File Programming, Finkel & Brown
Apple II™ Programming Exercises, Scanlon
8080/Z80 Assembly Language, Miller
*6502 Assembly Language Programming, Fernandez, Tabler, & Ashley
ATARI® BASIC, Albrecht, Finkel, & Brown
ATARI® Sound and Graphics, Moore, Lower, & Albrecht
Background Math for a Computer World, 2nd ed., Ashley
BASIC, 2nd ed., Albrecht, Finkel, & Brown
BASIC for Home Computers, Albrecht, Finkel, & Brown
*BASIC for the Apple II™, Brown, Finkel, & Albrecht
BASIC Programmer's Guide to Pascal, Borgerson
*Complete BASIC Dictionary, Adamis
Data File Programming in BASIC, Finkel & Brown
FAST BASIC: Beyond TRS-80™ BASIC, Gratzer
Flowcharting, Stern
FORTRAN IV, 2nd ed., Friedmann, Greenberg, & Hoffberg
*Fundamentals of Microcomputer Programming including Pascal, McGlynn
Golden Delicious Games for the Apple™ Computer, Franklin, Finkel,
    & Koltnow
How to Buy the Right Small Business Computer System, Smolin
Introduction to 8080/8085 Assembly Language Programming, Fernandez
    & Ashley
*Introduction to Computer Music, Bateman
Introduction to Data Processing, 2nd ed., Harris
Job Control Language, Ashley & Fernandez
*More Subroutine Sandwich, Grillo & Robertson
More TRS-80™ BASIC, Inman, Zamora, & Albrecht
Personal Computing, 2nd ed., McGlynn
Problem-Solving on the TRS-80™ Pocket Computer, Inman & Conlan
Structured COBOL, Ashley
*Subroutine Sandwich, Grillo & Robertson
TRS-80™ BASIC, Albrecht, Inman & Zamora
TRS-80™ Color BASIC, Albrecht
TRS-80™ Means Business, Lewis
*Useful Subroutines in BASIC, Adamis
Using CP/M, Fernandez & Ashley
*Using the TRS-80™ Model III, Finkel & Bove
Using Programmable Calculators for Business, Hohenstein
Why Do You Need A Personal Computer?, Leventhal & Stafford

*Forthcoming

Apple™ is a trademark of Apple Computer, Inc.
ATARI® is a registered trademark of Atari, Inc.
CP/M® is a registered trademark of Digital Research
TRS-80™ is a trademark of Tandy Corp.

A BASIC Programmer's Guide to Pascal

by

MARK J. BORGERSON

JOHN WILEY & SONS, INC.
NEW YORK   CHICHESTER   BRISBANE   TORONTO   SINGAPORE

Library of Congress Cataloging in Publication Data:

Borgerson, Mark J., 1946—
 A BASIC programmer's guide to Pascal.

 Includes index.
 1. PASCAL (Computer program language). 2. Basic (Computer program
language) I. Title. II. Title: B.A.S.I.C. programmer's guide to Pascal.
QA76.73.P2B65   001.64'24   81-16281
ISBN 0-471-09293-2   AACR2

Printed in the United States of America

82   83   9 8 7 6 5 4 3 2 1

TABLE OF CONTENTS

Preface   vii

Chapter   **Page**

 1 Living with the Revolution   1
 2 Elements of A Pascal Program   5
 3 Our First Building Blocks: Simple Data Tapes in Pascal and BASIC   13
 4 Scalar, Subrange and Set Variable Types   19
 5 Records and Arrays: Getting It All Together   28
 6 Typed Data Files   36
 7 The Other Kinds of Files   45
 8 Console and Printer Input and Output   51
 9 Control Structures   61
10 More on Program Structure   72
11 Getting Along with the System   81
12 And A Few Words in Closing   92

     Appendix I   Some Useful Procedures   99
     Appendix II   The Programmer's Cross Reference   112

PREFACE

This book is for all the programmers who were writing serious applications programs in BASIC, as I was, when we heard about a new language for microcomputers called Pascal. About two years ago I decided that I'd better find out about this stranger from the groves of academe. So I ran Pascal on my Apple II™* and started making mistakes. I learned Pascal the way many computer professionals and microcomputer users have to learn it— by reading books, manuals and magazine articles, and writing and running programs. As a result, I learned best those facets of the language used in applications programs—as opposed to academic exercises.

This book concentrates very heavily on data structures and program examples derived from actual business applications. This is not a textbook designed to teach an advanced student of computer science to write assemblers and compilers. Nor is it an introduction to the fundamental principles of computer science for the first-time programmer. It is written for the programmer with a good understanding of the capabilities and limitations of today's more advanced microcomputers.

Anyone reading this book becomes participant, willing or unwilling, in a revolution. This revolution is changing the way people learn, communicate, and interact with the world around them. The first "shots" in this revolution were fired in 1975 when a company named MITS sold a kit which enabled an individual to build his or her own computer. Since that time personal microcomputers like the Apple, Pet™, and TRS-80™ and IBM Personal Computer* have become firmly entrenched in our homes, schools and businesses.

Complete computer systems today are much more sophisticated than they were three years ago. Part of this sophistication is evident in the widespread use of floppy disk systems for program and data storage. Another, and less apparent, increase in capability is due to the *maturity* of

---

* APPLE II and the Apple Logo are registered trademarks of Apple Computers, Inc. PET is a registered trademark of Commodore Business Machines, Inc. TRS-80 is a registered trademark of the Tandy Corporation.

the software systems in use today. Professional microsystems programmers have now had several years to polish their products for the major microcomputer systems.

The software now available accomplishes a greater variety of tasks, is more "forgiving" of user errors, and is supported by better documentation—it is more *mature*. This maturation is not yet complete, however. The various brands of computers are still isolated. Part of the communication problem is due to differences in hardware and operating systems. Both the Apple II and Radio Shack TRS-80 use 5-¼" floppy disks for program and data storage, but the hardware for each system writes data to the diskette in a different manner. Thus a program diskette for one system cannot be read on the other.

For the micro-computer software market to mature completely, a language is needed that is understood by any microcomputer. This language would allow programs written for one computer to run on another — at least if the program didn't use hardware features not available on the second machine. The language should be clear, readable and concise so that programs could be modified to accommodate hardware differences and improved when possible. The current leader in the race to become the universal microcomputer language of the 1980's is UCSD Pascal* (the "UCSD" stands for University of California, San Diego).

UCSD Pascal is currently used for many microcomputers and should be available for all major brands in the next year. In fact, the availability of Pascal may become a major criterion in purchasing decisions of buyers in the years to come. Programs written in Pascal (from now on, unless otherwise noted, Pascal means UCSD Pascal) are readily transferred from one system to another. The language is clear, concise, and well-documented. Its biggest drawbacks are that it is relatively new and there are already thousands of programmers working in all those versions of BASIC.

It's time to begin the process of converting to Pascal programming. This book is not a complete how-to on the Pascal language—it is more like a travel guide. It's an exciting trip! This book points out some interesting sights—and warns of some hazards and annoyances. For really detailed information, study the Pascal system manuals and one or more references text on the Pascal language. This is definitely more of a business trip than a vacation, but don't let having to work along the way keep you from enjoying the journey from BASIC to Pascal.

---

* UCSD Pascal is a trademark of the Regents of the University of California.

1

Living with the Revolution

INTRODUCTION

The primary goal of this book is to take competent programmers in BASIC and teach them to apply what they've learned to a new language, Pascal. To do this we will examine the major differences between the two languages, using many examples and sample programs to show how similar problems are solved in each language.

By the time this book is finished, Pascal shouldn't be a foreign language, but a useful tool. It should have instilled enough confidence in the reader to enable him or her to use the reference manuals to start writing programs. The examples were chosen to illustrate the way BASIC routines are converted to Pascal. This book should also clarify the strengths of Pascal, making it easy to understand why it will be one of the dominant computer languages of the 1980s.

1

Pascal: The Background

Before jumping right into Pascal, it's helpful to have a little idea of its history. The Pascal language was developed by Kathleen Jensen and Niklaus Wirth in the early 1970's at the Institut fur Informatik in Zurich, Switzerland. The definitive document on the language, *Pascal User Manual and Report,* was published in 1974. By 1978, the Institute for Information Systems at the University of California's San Diego campus, under the leadership of Kenneth Bowles, had developed a Pascal operating system and compiler designed for use on mini- and microcomputers. The UCSD Pascal* system was originally marketed by the University of California. In 1979 the system became so popular that marketing and maintenance of programs consumed too much of the time of what was essentially a research group. As a result, all marketing rights were sold to Softech Microsystems—a San Diego software and systems house. Softech now markets versions of Pascal for all major mini- and microcomputers. The key elements of the UCSD Pascal system are:

Pascal Compiler.   Compiles the standard Pascal plus extensions for strings, random-access disk files, long integers, and graphics.

Text Editor.   An efficient, screen-oriented editor for the development of programs and for word-processing applications.

Assembler.   A sophisticated assembler capable of producing the machine code of the host processor.

Linker.   A linking loader for connecting separately compiled or assembled modules into a single program.

File Handling Utility.   A program for general-purpose file manipulation.

Utility Programs.   Programs for such functions as library maintenance and disk formatting.

As you can see from this list, the Pascal system is much more than just a compiler. In fact, the system provides all the programs needed to develop, test and maintain applications programs written in Pascal.

The key to the ability of UCSD Pascal to be run on many different systems lies in the fact that all major elements of the system have been written in Pascal. Many of the other operating systems available for microcomputers are written in machine language and cannot be run on a computer which uses a different microprocessor. The UCSD Pascal com-

---

* UCSD Pascal is a trademark of the Regents of the University of California.

piler produces code for a hypothetical machine...a processor optimized for the execution of Pascal code. This code (called pseudocode) is then interpreted by a short interpreter written in the machine language of the native processor. At least one manufacturer (Western Digital) is marketing a processor which directly executes the pseudocode. The use of pseudocode has both advantages and disadvantages. A major advantage is that to develop Pascal for a new processor, only the interpreter need be changed. Another advantage is that the pseudocode is very compact. The major disadvantage of the pseudocode approach is that the interpretation step causes programs to run two to three times slower than the same program would if it were compiled directly to the machine code of the host processor. But this is only a theoretical disadvantage since, even with pseudocode, the program still runs two to four times faster than the same program in BASIC.

BASIC: Choosing Our Dialect

In proceeding from BASIC to Pascal, the first thing to do is agree on the dialect of BASIC to be used as the starting point. Most of the examples in this book are written in Applesoft BASIC. This is the floating-point version of the language available on the Apple II™ personal computer. Applesoft is actually a version of an earlier BASIC distributed by Microsoft Incorporated, which has been extended to utilize the color graphics capabilities of the Apple II.

Since many other versions of BASIC treat string variables somewhat differently, some examples will refer to these other dialects. However, when there is no reference to a specific dialect of BASIC, assume that the example is written in Applesoft.

One area in which many versions of BASIC disagree is in the manner in which they define and use character strings. In Applesoft, a string array is defined with the statement DIM A$(10). This statement sets up storage for 11 different strings (subscripted from 0 to 10), each of which may be from 0 to 255 characters long. In Northstar BASIC the same statement would reserve space for only one string of 11 characters. This fundamental difference leads to very different methods of manipulating string information.

A second area in which most BASICs disagree is in the form of the statements to be used for input and output. These differences become most acute when we consider the form of statements used for reading and writing data files on floppy disks. Applesoft handles all Disk I/O by using PRINT statements with a special control character to notify the operating system that the data following is to be interpreted as a disk I/O command.

Other versions of BASIC contain special commands in the interpreter to handle the Disk I/O—usually by calling routines in the operating system.

Here is a nutshell comparison of BASIC and Pascal operating environments:

BASIC	Pascal
Interpreted Language	Compiled Language
Different Versions	One Version on Many
Different Computers	Different Computers
Two-character Variable Names	Long, Explanatory Names
Different Operating Systems	One Operating System on
Different Computers	All Computers

Where BASIC Is Still Best

There are still some areas where programming in BASIC still has its advantages. For small programs which will be run only a few times, the ability to write and run a program very quickly—without switching between the editor and the compiler—can give BASIC an edge. These are generally programs written by the person who uses them. People who continue to use BASIC are those doing their own programming to solve mathematical problems which change quite often, but do not require extremely complex programs for their solution. An example might be an engineer who writes a short program to compute and print a table of the strengths of a beam based on variations in two or three parameters. With the use of well-known equations and a simple FOR loop, the table could be printed in just a few minutes using BASIC. The same program could be written in Pascal, but the editing and compiling would take longer than writing the BASIC program; changing just one of the equations in the program would take much longer in Pascal.

BASIC will continue to have a place in very small systems. Today's microcomputers require one or more floppy disks to run Pascal. BASIC is now available in computers which fit handily into a coat pocket. No floppy disks are required for computers using BASIC—the interpreter, display memory and program memory all fit into the 64K memory space of the processor unit.

Finally, BASIC will have a place in those applications where good, well-documented programs have already been written which provide solutions to existing problems. If a particular problem has already been solved using a BASIC program, there is little point in rewriting the program in Pascal—except as an exercise to learn Pascal . . . which is what this book is all about.

2

The Elements of
a Pascal Program

In computer science circles, Pascal is referred to as a "structured" language. When this term is used by computer scientists, it means that the language requires certain regularities of format and program design. The term "structured" can also have many connotations, most of which have to do with the way in which programs are designed, written and run. Structured programs are generally composed of blocks of code which can be viewed as complete units independent of the program in which they are used. A Pascal procedure may be used in different programs without change, while a BASIC subroutine may have to use different line numbers and variable names in different programs. A structured programming language also places certain constraints on the manner in which control is transferred from one block to another. Pascal is more structured than BASIC because it places greater constraints on the transfer of control between procedures and other program elements. The structural elements of a Pascal program will be discussed briefly so that when these program elements are referred to later, it won't be confusing.

   BASIC programs are generally acknowledged to be less structured than Pascal programs. This is because the only main element of a BASIC program is a line of instructions which begins with an integer line number. Pascal programs don't require line numbers (listing produced when the program is compiled may include line numbers for reference purposes), but they do require certain program elements to be present and to occur in a certain order.

What's in A Name?

Every Pascal program begins with a program name statement:

```
PROGRAM PASCALDEMO (INPUT, OUTPUT);
```

This statement gives the program a name (which may be different from the file names used to save the source and object code) and defines two standard files, Input and Output, to be used with the program. UCSD Pascal assumes these two files to be present and to refer to the system console, so you won't always see that part of the program line. That part of the statement is a leftover from the time when Pascal programs were always run from batches of punch cards and each user had to request input and output devices specifically. Note that the statement is terminated with a semicolon, whereas a statement in BASIC is terminated by the carriage return at the end of a line. In fact, a Pascal statement may occupy several lines. Carriage returns and spaces within a program statement are generally ignored, although there are times when Pascal expects spaces to separate certain reserved words.

I Do Declare!

Immediately after the program name statement comes a series of statements collectively known as the DECLARATIONS section of the program. The declarations section contains a series of statements which define the constants, special types of data and the variables to be used in the program. Constant declarations must come first. The word CONST defines the start of this section. A list of constant values can then be given names and values:

```
CONST
    MAXNAME = 1000;
    NAMELENGTH = 25;
```

The first thing to note about this example is that the statements can be indented to show that they are part of the CONST declaration. In general, all examples in this book use indentations to show that a group of statements is included as a group within another logical unit.

Each constant is given a name, followed by an equals sign and a value. Items in the list are separated with semicolons. Only certain simple kinds of data, known as "simple data types," can be assigned as constants. These generally include integers, real numbers, characters and strings. In Pascal, even though the constants have names just like variables, they are true constants and remain fixed in value throughout a program. Attempting to assign a new value to a constant inside a program generates an error message.

Constant names can be long and self-explanatory in Pascal. UCSD Pascal only considers the first eight characters as significant, though, so all names, constants included, should be different somewhere in the first eight characters.

The next part of the declarations section is the TYPE definitions. This part of the program defines any special kinds of data to be used by the program. One of the greatest strengths of Pascal is its ability to define special data structures to fit the requirements of a particular application. A set of TYPE declarations might look like this:

```
TYPE
     NAMETYPE = STRING[25];
     MONTHNUM = 1 . . 12;
```

A whole chapter will be devoted to specially-defined data types, so further detail is unnecessary here.

The last part of the declarations section is the variable declarations. All global variables (those used throughout the whole program) must be defined in this section. BASIC allows you to define variables at any point in the program:

```
1000 X = 5
```

In BASIC, assignment of the value of five to the variable may be the first reference to the variable name. There is only one special variable, the *dynamic* type, which can be defined at any point in a Pascal program. Pascal requires that all other variable names and types be defined before they are used:

```
VAR
     X,Y:INTEGER;
     ANAME:STRING[25];
```

The key word VAR is followed by a list of names. Each name, or group of names, is followed by a colon and the type (either simple or defined in a TYPE statement) and terminated by a semicolon. When more than one variable is of the same type, they may be listed, separated by commas, before the colon as are the variables X and Y in the example above.

The "Performing" Blocks

The declarations are followed by the actual program block— statements that actually perform tasks the computer is to accomplish. A set of program statements in Pascal is always grouped within a BEGIN...END pair which defines the start and end of a logically connected group of statements. A very simple Pascal program, which uses no constants, special variable types or defined variables would look like this:

```
PROGRAM SIMPLEPRINT:
(* DECLARATIONS WOULD GO HERE *)
BEGIN
     WRITELN('THE PROGRAM HAS RUN');
END.
```

Any really useful program would, of course, have more than one statement between the BEGIN and the END. The main section of the program is always terminated with a period after the END statement.

Procedures

Pascal also has the ability to include special segments of program code which can be executed many times under the control of the main program segment. These blocks of program statements are called *procedures* and *functions*. A procedure is very much like a subroutine in a BASIC program. It is a block of code executed simply by referencing its name in the main program (or another procedure later in the program). In structure, a procedure looks much like a small Pascal program. It has its own name, a declarations section and a block of statements to be executed. The variables defined within a procedure are called *local* variables. The values of these variables, and even their names, are defined only while the program is actually executing the procedure. A simple procedure might look like this:

```
PROCEDURE SKIPLINES:
BEGIN
      WRITELN;
      WRITELN;
      WRITELN;
      WRITELN;
      WRITELN;
      WRITELN;
END;
```

This procedure would cause the program to write six blank lines to the console each time it was called. It is called by simply putting its name into the program at the point where you wish the procedure to be executed. In this case the name SKIPLINES would be used. There is no reserved word needed (like GOSUB in BASIC) to execute the procedure. A procedure call might look like this (ellipses indicate lines of code not needed in this example):

```
    . . . .
    . . . .
    . . . .(* PROGRAM STATEMENTS TO COLLECT SOME DATA *)
    . . . .
    PRINTDATA;
    SKIPLINES;
    . . . .
```

The PRINTDATA procedure could cause some data from a file to be displayed on the console, then the SKIPLINES procedure would separate that data from the next set with six blank lines.

Functions

A Pascal function is much like a defined function in BASIC. The function is invoked by simply using its name whenever you reach a point in the program where you need the actual result of the function. Here is a simple function:

```
FUNCTION UNITCOST:REAL;
BEGIN
     UNITCOST: = TOTALCOST/NUMBERUNITS;
END;
```

A function returns a value, which must be of a certain defined type. The type of value returned follows the colon in the function definition line. Somewhere inside the body of the function, a value is assigned to the function name itself.

As you may have noted, the operator in Pascal which assigns a value to a variable or function is the : = sequence. In BASIC the equals sign is used both to assign values and to denote a test for equality. In Pascal the equals sign is used only for the test for equality while the colon-equals sequence is used for value assignments.

The UNITCOST function could be called like this:

```
WRITELN('UNIT COST = ',UNITCOST);
```

Parameters

Both procedures and functions in Pascal can be sent special data items called *parameters* to use in their calculations. Parameters are enclosed inside parentheses right after the procedure or function name. The parameters in the definition must be defined as a particular TYPE, and the procedure call must pass only these types of data when the call is executed. Here is a procedure with parameters:

```
PROCEDURE SHOWNAME(ANAME:STRING);
BEGIN
     WRITELN(ANAME);
END;
```

and it would be called like this:

```
. . . .
SHOWNAME('JOHN SMITH');

. . . .
NEWNAME: = 'JANE DOE';
SHOWNAME(NEWNAME);
```

The second procedure call passed a variable, which must be a string variable. The WRITELN procedure which appeared in the above examples is a procedure built into the Pascal system (like the PRINT statement in BASIC). This procedure accepts string or character parameters and displays them on the console screen.

Parameters passed to a procedure may be either constants or variables.

```
OPENFILE('TRANSACTION.DATA');
and
OPENFILE(FILNAME);
```

are both valid procedure calls. The procedure definition would have a procedure name which would include the parameters:

```
PROCEDURE OPENFILE(FNAME:STRING);
```

The parameter used in the procedure call is known as the *actual* parameter. In this case it is also described as a "call by value" parameter. The parameter in the procedure definition is known as the *formal* parameter.

Procedures can also be defined with variable parameters in a manner which allows results to be passed back to the calling routine. The procedure call looks exactly the same, except that you cannot call the procedure with a constant parameter:

```
GETNAME(CLNAME,CLNUM);
```

However, there is a difference in the title line of the procedure itself:

```
PROCEDURE GETNAME(VAR NAME:STRING;
                  CNUM:INTEGER);
```

The word VAR before the name parameter notifies the compiler that the following parameter is the *address* of the data to be used in the procedure calculations. The procedure works with the data contained in the address, and may modify that data as well as simply read it for use inside the procedure itself. Parameters defined in this manner are called "call by name" parameters. The procedure might work like this:

```
PROCEDURE GET NAME(VAR NAME:STRING;
                        CNUM:INTEGER);
BEGIN
    SEEK(NAMEFIL,CNUM);
    GET(NAMEFIL);
    NAME: = NAMEFIL^;
END;
```

In this case the name read from the file would be passed back to the calling routine. The way in which the Input/Output (I/O) statements work will be explained in a later chapter.

The preceding material covers the main elements of a Pascal program. The following chapters discuss these elements in greater detail. If programs are to be quickly and correctly written, easily maintained and useful to someone else, the programmer may have to think about problems in a slightly different way. BASIC allows a programming problem to be attacked in a haphazard manner—writing code, testing, redefining data, then rewriting the code. The strength of BASIC in allowing rapid changes in programs and data structures can become a disadvantage. It can be too easy to think of a program as a structure that doesn't have to be correctly designed before it is built. Pascal also allows programming problems to be approached this way, but only at a very high price. That price is measured in terms of time. Since Pascal is a compiled language, each change in a program or one of its data structures requires that the program be edited and recompiled. This takes much longer than changing one statement in a BASIC program. Therefore, Pascal places a much higher premium on thinking before writing.

My advice at this point is to try writing some programs while reading this book, without trying to finish a complete general ledger package. In order to complete any really complex programs, a good grasp of all the building blocks of Pascal covered in this book is needed. It is also necessary to spend quite a bit of time thumbing through the reference manuals for your particular brand of Pascal. The next chapters concentrate on making the building blocks of Pascal a little more familiar.

3

Our First Building Blocks: Simple Data Types in Pascal and Basic

Any computer language must have certain fundamental data elements from which data structures of interest to the programmer are built. These data elements are the simple data types of the language. The vast majority of today's microcomputers use the 8-bit byte as the most primitive data type. When programming one of these microcomputers in assembly language, individually-addressed bytes of data are manipulated. Some microprocessors, such as the Z-80, allow the programmer to set or clear single bits individually within a memory byte. But even in this case the programmer must specify the byte upon which the operation is to take place.

A new generation of microprocessors is now reaching the market, manipulating data directly in 16- or 32-bit words. In some cases, the 32-bit words can be treated as floating point numbers with an 8-bit exponent and

13

a 24-bit mantissa. However, it will probably be a year or two before these processors show up in consumer products. For now, consider the 8-bit byte the most primitive data structure for today's microcomputers. So, when programming a microcomputer in assembly language, any other data types must be defined in terms of groups of one or more bytes.

Both BASIC and Pascal allow the programmer to use more complex data elements as the simple types. They do this by hiding from the programmer those operations needed to build the simple types from the 8-bit bytes or 16-bit words actually used by the computer. Here are the simple types available to BASIC and Pascal programmers:

BASIC	Pascal
Integer	Integer
Real	Real
. . . . . .	Boolean
. . . . . .	Char
String	String (UCSD Pascal only)

As you can see, Pascal has two simple types that are not available in most BASICs. In addition, different versions of BASIC have differing definitions of the simple types. In order to get this all straightened out, we'll have to consider each of these simple types in a little more detail.

Integers: Counting with 16 Fingers

An integer is a number without a fractional part. When programming in BASIC, it's typical to be upset at least once by fractional parts that disappear when one integer is divided by another. Both Pascal and BASIC agree that an integer shall occupy 16 bits, or two bytes, of memory space. A 16-bit integer can assume values from -32768 to +32767. This is only a small part of all the possible integers, of course. (Asking a mathematician how small a part it is will produce a long discourse on the variations in infinity.) When a value is limited to a particular range, someone always needs a value just a little bit larger or smaller. For instance, the publisher of a popular national magazine would soon run into trouble if the number of issues sold was stored as an integer. (UCSD Pascal could keep them out of trouble with long integers—integers which can have values with as many as 36 digits—but since the length of the integer must be specified by the programmer, the data type is not a simple type.)

Real Numbers: Really Big and Really Small

The numbers used most often in everyday BASIC programming are real numbers. This often comes about because any number is assumed to be a real number unless the programmer specifies it to be an integer. A real number consists of an integer part, a fractional part, and an exponent. When BASIC or Pascal prints out a real number, the fractional part is zero (that is, if the number could be represented as an integer). The exponent part is usually printed only if the number is too large or too small to be represented exactly in the BASIC. Different versions of BASIC store real sion of BASIC. Different versions of BASIC store real numbers in varying manners.

Applesoft and many other versions of BASIC store numbers internally in pure binary format. A conversion routine is then required to convert the numbers from their internal format to the decimal display format. This routine may cause some round-off errors for numbers which are near to the limits of precision of the variable. However, there is an advantage to this pure binary format. Microcomputers are best at doing arithmetic operations in this format and can often do many calculations several times faster in this mode.

Those versions of BASIC, like Cromemco 16K BASIC, which use BCD (Binary-Coded Decimal) arithmetic can use a much simpler conversion routine to change the internal format to the printed format. Any number within the numeric range of the variable can be represented without round-off error. This type of arithmetic has its own disadvantages, though. First, it is usually slower to carry out calculations in BCD format. Secondly, a BCD-coded variable has a smaller numeric range than a binary-coded variable occupying the same number of bytes. For example, if we allocate two bytes for the mantissa of a number, the maximum usable BCD number is 9999 since each byte can store only two decimal digits. A two-byte binary number can be large as 65,535 (ignoring for the moment the fact that we have to steal a bit somewhere for the sign if we want negative numbers). Perhaps the most important thing to remember about real numbers is that there are many different representations in currently popular versions of BASIC. This leads us to our first warning:

WARNING

When converting a program from BASIC to Pascal, be sure that the real variables do not require more significant digits than are available in Pascal. If the program uses dollar and cent amounts greater than $9999.99, consider using long integers and keeping track of everything in cents.

Boolean Variables: "Maybe" Not Allowed

A data element which can have one of two possible values, true or false, is a Boolean variable (named after English mathematician George Boole). Boolean variables are not available in BASIC, even though most versions of BASIC allow you to treat an integer value as if it were a Boolean variable. In Pascal, a Boolean value is stored in a 16-bit word, but only the least significant bit is actually used to store information. Boolean variables are most often used in testing control conditions within a program in conjunction with an IF statement.

In BASIC, Boolean expressions are used to control program flow just as they are used in Pascal, without the same capability to store the result of a Boolean expression for later reference. BASIC generally evaluates Boolean expressions as numeric expressions internally, then sets the result to TRUE if the expression evaluates to zero and FALSE if the result is not zero. Thus in some BASIC programs there may be lines like:

```
120     IF A THEN 150
```

which would cause the program to branch to line 150 whenever A is not zero.

One last note—generally, the value of a Boolean variable cannot be directly printed out. The UCSD Pascal system "dislikes" printing out the words TRUE and FALSE, so a program element such as a CASE statement (which will be discussed later) must be added. This is much the same as in BASIC, where the value of a Boolean expression becomes a number—zero if the expression is false and one if it is true.

CHAR Variables

Both BASIC and Pascal often need to manipulate single ASCII characters. Pascal allows this with the CHAR type. Each CHAR variable stores a single character in one 16-bit word. BASIC requires that characters be treated either as strings only one character long or that they be manipulated by reference to their numeric order in the ASCII character sequence. Both languages have built-in functions which allow the programmer to manipulate character information by referring to the numeric position of the character in the ASCII character set. Here are the BASIC and Pascal equivalent functions:

BASIC	Pascal	Function
ASC("X")	ORD('X')	returns the integer
ASC(I$)	ORD(ACHAR)	which represents the position of the character in the ASCII sequence.
CHR$(49)	CHR(49)	returns the character
CHR$(I)	CHR(INTVAL)	having the position in the ASCII sequence represented by the integer argument.

Note that since BASIC uses a string argument in the ASC function, it will only examine the first character of the string. A second point to note is that when a constant argument of the CHAR or string is being specified in Pascal, a single quote (') or apostrophe is used to delimit the character, while BASIC uses the standard double quote.

Strings

The ability to manipulate textual information is very important in any computer language. Pascal, as originally defined by Jensen and Wirth, did not include a simple data type for the manipulation of character strings. UCSD Pascal has added the string type to allow easier manipulation of variable-length character strings. A string variable is a packed array of characters, each of which occupies one byte of storage. A string variable may have a maximum length of 255 characters in Pascal, but unless it is set by the programmer, maximum length assumes a default value of 80 characters. The maximum length of 255 characters results from the fact that each string has a single byte associated with it which is used to store the current length of the string; 255 is the largest number that may be stored in a single byte.

The most common dialects of BASIC are about evenly divided on how strings are handled. For the moment these two types will be referred to as S1 and S2 BASICs. Type S1 BASIC treats each string as an individual entity and uses special string functions to manipulate the characters within the string. Applesoft and Microsoft BASIC are examples of type S1 BASICs. Type S2 BASICs treat a string as if it were an array of characters. Individual characters within the string are manipulated by referring to the character as if it were an array element. Type S1 strings are generally limited to about 255 characters in length—as are Pascal strings. Strings in type S2 BASICs are usually limited only by the available memory of the computer.

The limited length of strings in type S1 BASICs is generally compensated for by the fact that you can declare arrays of strings. For instance the statement

```
10 DIM A$(100)
```

reserves storage for 101 different strings, each of which can be up to 255 characters in length. In a type S2 BASIC the same statement would reserve storage for a single string of 100 characters maximum length.

It is easy to see by now that Pascal combines the features of type S1 and S2 strings. Pascal strings follow the convention of S2 strings in that a declaration such as

```
TYPE
    ASTRING = STRING[100];
```

reserves space for a single string with a maximum length of 100 characters. Pascal also allows manipulation of the individual characters of the string by specifying the position of the character within the string. Manipulations of this type should be attempted with caution. If you meddle with the 80th character of the string when only 50 characters have been read into the string variable, you will get unexpected results. Pascal also allows the programmer to specify arrays of strings in much the same manner as type S1 BASICs. The declaration

```
VAR
    CITYNAMES:ARRAY[1..20] OF ASTRING
```

reserves storage for 20 strings, each of which can be up to 100 characters long.

The rest of this book assumes familiarity with the handling of strings in type S1 BASICs. Most of the examples of string manipulations are written in Applesoft BASIC.

4

Scalar, Subrange and Set Variable Types

This chapter looks at three special types of variables. Scalar variables are used in Pascal whenever data can be separated into a limited (and well-known) number of categories. Subrange variables are used when working with either numbers or categories, without needing or wanting to use the whole range of possible values in a category. Set variables are a type of subrange variables upon which certain special operations may be performed. Using these variable types can make programs more readable and help avoid fundamental errors in handling certain variables. These variable types are not available in BASIC, but are often approximated with one or more manipulations of integer data.

Scalar Types: Pick One From Category A

A scalar type in Pascal is a data type which represents an element of data which can be put into one of a fixed number of categories. The simplest example of a scalar might be something like this:

19

```
VAR
     SELECTION:CHAR;
```

Variables of the type CHAR are scalar variables because the possible values are limited in number and have a distinct order of occurrence. Another useful scalar type is the *enumeration*. With variables of this type we must define each of the possible values. The Pascal compiler then keeps track of the name of each of the enumeration variables and their order of occurrence. For instance, we might have the following type which represents a person's profession:

```
VAR
     PROFESSION: (TINKER,TAILOR,SOLDIER,SAILOR,
                  BEGGAR,THIEF);
```

With this statement we have strictly limited the professions a person can pursue—at least as far as our computer is concerned. Moreover, each person must be assigned one of these professions—there is no "none of the above" fudging allowed. Of course we could add the category UNDECIDED to the list as a catch-all. A profession may now be assigned with a simple statement such as:

```
PROFESSION: = TINKER;
```

To achieve the same results in BASIC it would be necessary to use REM statements to associate each profession with an integer value. This might be done as follows:

```
10 REM PROFESSIONS ARE REPRESENTED BY THE INTEGER PF%
20 REM
30 REM FOR TINKER PF% = 1
 ·0 REM FOR TAILOR PF% = 2
50 REM FOR SOLDIER PF% = 3
60 REM FOR SAILOR PF% = 4
70 REM FOR BEGGAR PF% = 5
80 REM FOR THIEF PF% = 6
90 REM
100  PF% = 1
110 REM SET PROFESSION AS TINKER
```

(The percent sign denotes an integer variable in Applesoft and many other BASICs.)

As a matter of fact, Pascal stores the scalar variable internally as an integer just as is done in the BASIC example. However, the compiler automatically replaces the written name with the integer value. The first name is replaced with the number one, the second name with two, the third with three, and so on. The result is that the Pascal program lets you have clear, well-documented code without the overhead of all the REM statements. Remember that in the BASIC program the REM statements take up memory space and slow down the execution. The Pascal compiler also checks to make sure that scalar variables are not defined which are outside the set ranges. It also makes sure that variable types are not mixed in the program. After the Pascal program is compiled, all the long scalar names are reduced to simple positive integers, which use less space and are processed faster.

Another important characteristic of scalar variables is that they are *ordered* in the sequence of their definition. Suppose a scalar type is defined to represent military ranks:

```
VAR
    RANK:(LIEUTENANT,CAPTAIN,MAJOR,LTCOLONEL,
        COLONEL,BRIGADIER);
```

Somewhere in a program we have define a rank as follows:

```
RANK: = CAPTAIN;
```

A little later in the program we find that it is time for a promotion. Pascal does not allow use of the statement:

```
RANK: = RANK + 1;
```

since the ranks are not supposed to be thought of in terms of numbers. In BASIC, it would probably just say:

```
RN% = RN% + 1: REM INCREASE RANK BY 1.
```

However, Pascal does give us a built-in function to accomplish this promotion. The SUCC and PRED (for successor and predecessor) functions allow a scalar variable to be moved either up or down one step, respectively. To promote our captain we use the statement:

```
RANK: = SUCC(RANK);
```

The Pascal compiler also checks each assignment of a value to a scalar type as the program is compiled. Thus the statement:

RANK: = ADMIRAL;

would result in an error message when the program was compiled, since the rank of admiral is not one of the defined possibilities in the scalar variable. BASIC does not check the values assigned to an integer representing a category, so it is possible (generally by forgetting what the variable represents) to write:

10 RN% = 3: REM SET RANK AS MAJOR

then later,

5890 RN% = RN%*3

which not only produces a value out of the allowable range, but also puts the programmer in the somewhat ridiculous position of having defined something which is three times a major. The Pascal compiler stresses that it is not permissible to use numeric operations on scalar variables, so this type of mistake would not be allowed. In addition, the run-time module of the Pascal system halts the program, calling attention to the error if the value of the scalar variable is outside the accepted range. This would occur in the execution of the statement:

RANK: = SUCC(RANK);

when the rank was already defined as brigadier. Thus in both BASIC and Pascal it is up to the programmer to make sure that a statement is not executed that would put a variable into an undefined category. Both languages allow the mistake, but only Pascal stops the program if it occurs.

Just as BASIC won't print out the word "brigadier" if you say:

100 PRINT RN%

Pascal loses the connection between the rank BRIGADIER and the word "brigadier" when the program is compiled. Thus if you try to compile the statement:

WRITE(RANK);

you get a "Variable Type error" message since scalar variables cannot be directly printed out. We get around this in the same way we did with Boolean variables:

```
CASE RANK OF
    LIEUTENANT:WRITE('LIEUTENANT');
    CAPTAIN:WRITE('CAPTAIN');
    MAJOR:WRITE('MAJOR');
    LTCOLONEL:WRITE('LIEUTENANT COLONEL');
    COLONEL:WRITE('COLONEL');
    BRIGADIER:WRITE('BRIGADIER GENERAL');
END; (*OF CASE STATEMENT*)
```

In BASIC we would probably use ON RN% GOTO 2020, 2030, 2040...etc. to jump to a line which would print each rank.

Subrange Variables: Pick Any Card— As Long As It's A Heart

There are many times when we may want to use a variable to represent a certain portion of the range of another variable type. The Pascal subrange variable provides a neat, concise way to accomplish this goal. The variable type which represents the whole range of values is called the "base type." Suppose, as in the example above, the categories of military officers have been defined. Now we wish to define another variable representing only field-grade officers (Lieutenant Colonel through Brigadier). First, define the base type of the subrange:

```
TYPE
    RANK = (LIEUTENANT,CAPTAIN,MAJOR,LTCOLONEL,
    COLONEL,BRIGADIER);
```

Then define another type of variable to be a subrange of this variable:

```
FIELDGRADE = LTCOLONEL..BRIGADIER;
```

The fieldgrade type can now have only those values from Lieutenant Colonel through Brigadier. The two periods tell the compiler to accept all values from the beginning subrange type to the value after the two periods. Both compile-time and run-time range checking are performed on subranges just as they are on scalar values.

A subrange variable may also be used to define a range of integers or characters. Thus for a program using dates, the following subranges might be defined:

```
MONTH = 1 . . 12;
DAY = 1 . . 31;
YEAR = 0 . . 99;
```

The base type of these variables is the simple type—integer.

We can also define subranges of the base type CHAR. For instance the subrange type:

```
SELECTION = 'A' . . 'F';
```

might be used to define a variable which is the answer to a multiple-choice test question. Here we are limited to six of the 128 ASCII characters.

Subrange types are internally stored as integers, just like scalar variables. Since one integer represents each of the values in the subrange, a subrange of real number values cannot be defined. Imagine how many integers it would take to represent each possible real value between 1.00000 and 10.0000. The Pascal compiler halts with an error message if a subrange is defined:

```
EXECSALARY = 40000.00 . . 100000.00;
```

BASIC has no true equivalent to the subrange variable type. It would be required to check each variable value at run time to see if it is in a subrange. Of course, this type of checking is also required in Pascal when asking for user input. If you are looking for a character to assign to a variable of the subrange type SELECTION defined above and the user enters a 'Z', the program will come to a crashing halt unless the character is rejected before it is assigned to the variable. A BASIC program would not halt without checking the range before assigning the variable, but a later attempt to use that 'Z' might get very strange results.

In Pascal programs, subrange variables are often used in defining other structures such as SETS and RECORDS. The use of subranges can result in significant savings in memory space, as is evident when examining the PACKED RECORD data structure. Another advantage of subranges is that the name given to the subrange can be very helpful in reminding the programmer exactly what part of a larger range of variables is represented by the data. Thus, with the following definitions:

```
DAYNAMES = (MONDAY,TUESDAY,WEDNESDAY,
            THURSDAY,FRIDAY,SATURDAY,SUNDAY);
WEEKEND = SATURDAY . . SUNDAY;
```

one is unlikely to assign a value of TUESDAY to a variable of type WEEKEND. This is another good example of how Pascal allows the structuring of data and programs in a way that helps reduce programming errors. In this example, the names for Thursday through Sunday are indented to make it easier to find the DAYNAMES definition and to show that the specific names are part of the definition.

Sets: But No Games Or Rackets

A special data type available in Pascal which has no analog in BASIC is the SET type. The simplest way to think of a SET is to consider it as a basket. This basket can hold up to 512 items and all the items must be of the same fundamental type. (The limitation of 512 items as the size of the basket is an implementation restriction of UCSD Pascal.) Since each item in the set will be represented by a single bit in the set variable, and there are a fixed number of bits available, a set can include only items which can be represented by zero and positive integers less than 512. Thus sets may be made up of variables of the integer, CHAR, or scalar types, and subranges of the integer or scalar type. You cannot define a set of real values for the same reason you cannot define a subrange from 1.0 to 2.0—there is an infinite number of them! A set is defined with either a TYPE or VAR statement. For example:

```
TYPE MONTHNAME   = (JAN,FEB,MAR,APR,MAY,JUN,JUL
                    AUG,SEP,OCT,NOV,DEC);
     SEASON          = SET OF MONTHNAME;
     YEARQUARTER = SET OF 1..12;
VAR  SUMMER          :SEASON;
     LASTQUARTER  :YEARQUARTER;
```

In this example, the abbreviated name of the month is defined as a scalar variable type. We have then defined a set variable type, SEASON, which can hold none, some or all of the possible month names. The definition of the quarter-year set did not require a preceding type declaration since the set is made up of a subrange of the fundamental type integer. We could, however, have defined the month numbers a little differently:

```
TYPE    MONTHNUM    = 1..12;
        YEARQUARTER  = SET OF MONTHNUM
```

We have now defined a subrange type which is the number of the month and then used that subrange in the set definition. The second definition is clearer—if only because we have associated the numbers from 1 to 12 with month numbers. Once the set types are defined, memory space can be reserved for a variable of the set type with the VAR statement. At this point we have built our baskets and decided what type of items they may hold, without deciding exactly what is in the basket. To define the contents of the basket we have to put some specific items in it. We do this with an assignment statement and a special expression known as a *set constructor:*

SUMMER : = [JUN, JUL, AUG];

The set constructor is started with the left bracket, then includes the items to be in the set separated by commas and is terminated with the right bracket. When the set is defined each bit corresponding to a month name within the constructor is set to a Boolean TRUE. The bits corresponding to all the other month names are set to FALSE. In this definition, the summer season is defined to include only the months of June, July and August.

In order to illustrate some of the operations possible with sets, a few more set variables are needed, all of the type SEASON.

VAR   RAINYSEASON,DRYSEASON,WHOLEYEAR:SEASON;
      MONTH:MONTHNAM:
      TESTVALUE:BOOLEAN

Now we'll set up some initial values:

WHOLEYEAR   : =   [JAN..DEC];
DRYSEASON   : =   [MAY..SEP];
RAINYSEASON   : =   [JAN...APR,OCT..DEC];
MONTH   : =   FEB;

We will begin with the most often used and most useful set operator—the IN operator. This operator tests whether a particular element is part of a set. The IN operator might be used as follows:

TESTVALUE : = MONTH IN DRYSEASON;

In this case TESTVALUE would be assigned the Boolean value FALSE since the month (February) is not in the dry season. To return to the original analogy, the IN operator simply reveals whether a given item is in the basket which comprises a particular set.

The next most useful set operator is the UNION operator. This operator, invoked with the + sign, gives back a set which contains all of the items which were in the two sets on either side of the plus sign. This operator could be used to change the definition of the rainy season as follows:

RAINYSEASON: = RAINYSEASON + [MAY];

The month of May is now added to the set of rainy months. Please note the brackets around MAY, since the + operator works with two *sets*. Without the brackets, MAY is an *element* of a set, and not a true set.

Two other set operators, the *intersection* of two sets, invoked with a * and the *difference*, invoked with a −, are also defined but less often used. The intersection of two sets results in a set which contains only those elements present in *both* sets. If we used the example sets (after adding May to the rainy season) and carried out the following operation:

DAMPMONTHS : = RAINYSEASON * DRYSEASON;

the set of damp months would contain only May, since that is the only month name that appears in both the rainy and dry seasons.

The difference operator produces a set which contains all those elements present in the set before the minus sign and not present in the set after the sign. It essentially allows you to remove from the first set all those elements present in the second set. I recommend consulting a good book on set theory before using these operations.

Set operations are very useful in conjunction with sets of characters. When we look at different ways to collect user input from the terminal and check for illegal characters, we will make extensive use of sets of characters and the + and IN operators.

5

Records and Arrays: Getting It All Together

The power of Pascal becomes very evident when forming definitions of the kinds of data structures found in complex business and scientific programs. The record structure is used to group several different types of data into a single structure. An array is a group of data items which are all of the same type. While the array structure is available in BASIC, that language has nothing quite like the Pascal record. Since we'll be exploring some completely new concepts, it's time for a little basic training in multiple-word data structures.

Records: "All Right Youse Guys, Fall In and Move Out Together!"

One of the most powerful features of Pascal is the data RECORD. A record is a group of data items organized into a single logical unit. There is no exact analog to the record structure in BASIC. The closest you can get is an array used to associate several related numbers. Even then, much of the power of the record structure is missing. A record is defined by giving it a name, then listing the components, which may be either simple data types or previously-defined complex data types. A simple record which defines an item in a business inventory program might look like this:

```
TYPE
    INVITEM = RECORD
            NAME : STRING[20];
            COST : REAL;
            ONHAND : INTEGER;
            ONORDER : INTEGER;
        END;
VAR
    NEWITEM,SALEITEM:INVITEM;
```

Now we have defined an inventory record which has four separate parts and uses three different variable types. We can define as many variables as we want to be of this type. To assign a value to one of the components of the record we use the name of the record, then the name of the component, separated by a period. In the process of initializing an inventory record we might make the following assignments:

```
NEWITEM.NAME: = 'NEW ITEM';
NEWITEM. COST: = 0.00;
NEW ITEM. ONHAND: = 0;
NEW ITEM. ONORDER: = 10;
```

If the record were more complex, consisting of about 20 parts, it might get very tiresome typing out the NEWITEM. part of the component name. Pascal has a special facility to simplify the tasks of working with components of a single record. The WITH operator allows us to specify that we are working with a particular record variable and thereafter omit the name of the variable in program statements. It is used like this:

```
WITH NEWITEM DO
    BEGIN
        NAME: = 'NEW ITEM';
        COST: =0.00;
        ONHAND: = 0;
        ONORDER: =10;
    END:   (*OF 'WITH NEWITEM' *)
```

Looking back at this example, it serves as an introduction to two new features of Pascal. The first of these is the *compound statement*. A compound statement is a set of simple statements grouped together with a BEGIN . . . END sequence. Simple statements are almost always indented from the BEGIN and END to show that they are logically grouped together. When a series of compound statements is nested within a program, the indentation becomes absolutely necessary if the program structure is to be understood. This matter of program structure and format will be discussed much more thoroughly in a later chapter.

The second new feature is the Pascal equivalent of the BASIC REM statement. In Pascal the text enclosed within the (* . . . *) pairs or within { }(which may or may not be available—they aren't on the standard Apple) are treated as comments which are not compiled. Thus these comments are available in the source code to help readers understand the program, but they do not take up space in the compiled program. The REM statements in a BASIC program not only take up memory space in the running program, but they may slow up the program execution to some degree.

Pascal provides an even more powerful tool when working with records—all the components of a record can be transferred without ever referring to the component by name! To make the SALEITEM variable equal to the NEWITEM variable, for example, the transfer of the data from one to the other is as simple as:

SALEITEM: = NEWITEM;

Pascal treats the record as a single logical unit. You can pass the record as a parameter to a function or procedure or set it equal to another variable (of the same record type) simply by using its name. Compare the simple statement above to its BASIC equivalent:

```
110   SN$ = NN$ : REM TRANSFER NAMES
120   SC = NC : REM TRANSFER COST
130   SH = NH : REM NUMBER ON HAND
140   SO = NO : REM NUMBER ON ORDER
```

If the record had 15 to 20 components, an element-by-element transfer would get very tedious.

Packed Records: "All Right, Close It Up, Youse Guys!"

There is another feature of the record structure that can be very useful in working with programs which use large data arrays. This feature is the *packed record*. A packed record is one in which the elements are compressed into the minimum number of computer words. In UCSD Pascal the unit of storage is the 16-bit word. A packed record uses only as much storage as is required for a particular component of the record. Integer and real variables use exactly one and two words of storage, respectively, so there is no advantage to be gained by defining a packed record which contains only these types of components. Subrange and scalar variables, though, may require much less than a whole word of storage. Consider the following variable types:

```
TYPE
    VEHTYPE = (CAR,TRUCK,MOTORCYCLE,BICYCLE);
    NUMWHEELS = 1..18;

    VEHICLE = PACKED RECORD
        WHATKIND: VEHTYPE;
        WHEELS:NUMWHEELS;
    END;
```

Since there are only four possible types of vehicle, that scalar can be represented with only 2 bits of data. The number of wheels can be represented with 5 bits of information, since 5 bits can represent values from 0 to 31. Thus the packed record could be represented in only 7 bits of storage. The Pascal system does not like to work with units of data other than complete words, so the packed record would actually use a full 16-bit word, with 9 bits remaining unused. When using packed records which occupy more than one word of storage, the system always reserves an integral number of words for each record. Thus, in many cases, all the data storage space is not used to 100% efficiency. But, when properly used, packed records can greatly decrease the amount of storage used for certain types of records.

As an example of an effective use of packed records, consider a variable which is used quite often in business programs—a date. A date in the form 10/23/81 is actually three separate numbers; the month, the day, and year. Each of these numbers can have only certain values. Consider the following record structure:

```
TYPE
  MONTH = 1 . . 12;
  DAY = 1 . . 31;
  YEAR = 0 . . 99;

  DATE = PACKED RECORD;
    MM:MONTH;
    DD:DAY;
    YY:YEAR;
  END;
```

In this example, the month requires four bits, the day 5 bits, and the year 7 bits. Total storage required is only 16 bits, or one word. This is one-third the storage that would be needed if the record were not packed. In BASIC, three integers would be needed to maintain the date, or it would be necessary to pack the data numerically with a formula like:

```
100 DT = 10000*Y1 + 100*M1 + D1
```

The result is certainly less efficient than the Pascal packed record.

There are certain restrictions placed on the use of packed records in UCSD Pascal. A component of a packed record cannot be passed by itself as a parameter to a function or a procedure. Thus, if a function checks the year of a transaction, you must pass the complete date as a parameter, then refer to the year component within the function definition. This restriction is generally not a problem if packed records are used where they will actually save a lot of storage rather than as a general principle.

A second disadvantage of the packed record is that it does take the computer some time to pack and unpack the record when the components are being read or modified. UCSD Pascal automatically packs and unpacks the record each time a component is referenced. In standard Pascal there are functions called PACK and UNPACK which allow unpacking a record, modifying one or more components, then packing the record again. Thus, three components can be modified with just a single unpack and pack sequence instead of the three sequences that would be used in UCSD Pascal.

WARNING

Packed records are not implemented in the same manner in all Pascal systems. In addition, there are differences in the way in which packed records which themselves contain packed records are handled. Check the system manual for details pertinent to your Pascal system.

ARRAYS: "You're All BOOTS to Me!"

Pascal allows much the same facilities for defining array structures as does BASIC. Where a DIM statement is used in BASIC, an ARRAY declaration is used in Pascal. The following statements would produce the same type of arrays in the two languages:

```
100 DIM A(100) : REM 101 (0-100) REAL NUMBERS
110 DIM B$(50) : REM 51 DIFFERENT STRINGS IN APPLESOFT
120 DIM C%(20,20) : REM 21 BY 21 MATRIX OF INTEGERS
```

```
VAR
  A          :  ARRAY[0..100] OF REAL;
  BSTRINGS   :  ARRAY[0..50] OF STRING;
  CMATRIX    :  ARRAY[0..20,0..20] O INTEGER;
```

Note that brackets, [and], are used to enclose the array index in Pascal, rather than the parentheses used in BASIC.

In Pascal, arrays are fixed in size when the program is compiled. In BASIC a number from the console can often be read when the program is run, then using that number to dimension an array. For instance:

```
200 INPUT "HOW MANY DATA ITEMS?";ND
210 DIM DA(ND) : REM SET UP THE ARRAY.
```

This can lead to problems if an inexperienced operator decides that there are going to be 10,000 data items. At five bytes per real value, this means 50,000 bytes of storage—and Applesoft doesn't leave quite that much room for variable storage. Pascal requires defining the array before the program is run—make it too big, and the program will screech to a halt with a STACK OVERFLOW message as soon as it is run. (It will compile OK, though.)

In both Pascal and BASIC, the designer of the program should know before the program is written how large any data arrays will become. The arrays are then defined to include this maximum number of items and any indexes into the arrays are tested to be sure they are within the allowed range. In Pascal it is convenient and clear to use a constant declaration at the beginning of the program to define the sizes of important arrays:

```
CONST
  MAXFOLIO = 60 (*MAXIMUM # ITEMS IN PORTFOLIO*)

TYPE
  TRANSREC = RECORD
      NUMSHARES:INTEGER;
      PURDATE:DATE;
      STOCKNAME:STRING[25];
      TOTALCOST:INTEGER[8];
  END;

VAR
  PORTFOLIO = ARRAY[0..MAXFOLIO] OF TRANSREC;
```

Here we have a good example of the powerful data structuring capability of Pascal. We have an array of specially-defined records, each of which represents a transaction in the stock market. This data structure would be extremely difficult to represent in BASIC, but is well defined and straightforward in Pascal. We can modify the stock name of the first element in the array with a statement like:

```
PORTFOLIO[0].STOCKNAME := 'FORD MOTOR CO.'
```

The elements of this array can be treated exactly like any other variable of the type TRANSREC.

Pascal also allows manipulation of complete arrays as if they were single variables. Consider the following example:

```
TYPE
  TRANSARRAY = ARRAY[0..MAXTRANS] OF TRANSREC;

VAR
  OLDSTOCK, CURRENTSTOCK:TRANSARRAY;
```

Assuming that some data has been read into the current stock array (from a disk file—which has not been discussed yet) we can then make a backup copy of the data with the statement:

```
OLDSTOCK:=CURRENTSTOCK;
```

With this single statement all the elements in the current stock array have been copied to their corresponding elements in the old stock array.

Packed Arrays: "Close It Up, Soldiers!"

Pascal also allows an array to be defined as a PACKED ARRAY. Packed arrays are much like packed records in that the data will be compressed into the fewest number of words possible. Since most data structures in UCSD Pascal will already be several words long, packed arrays have only a limited usefulness in most business programs. However, many of the text and reference books on the market today use a lot of examples of packed arrays of CHAR. This is because Standard Pascal does not allow the string variable type and many large computers using Pascal have words of 32- or 60-bits length. Using unpacked arrays of characters means using a 60-bit word to store a character that could be contained in 7 bits. Since most users of BASIC are already familiar with strings, I'll concentrate on them as a manner of handling alphanumeric information. A string is essentially a packed array of characters which has an associated length parameter. It is possible to refer to the elements of a string as if they were array elements. Thus the statement

```
ACHAR: = ASTRING[5]
```

is a perfectly valid way to refer to the fifth element of the variable ASTRING. It is also an easy way to get into trouble if ASTRING happens to be only four characters long. It is possible to reference characters past the actual length of the string without generating any error message—so be careful when treating strings as arrays of characters.

Packed arrays may be useful in working with subrange variables of limited size (numbers less than 255). The Pascal system will not allow a packed array element to cross a word boundary, so it won't help to try to pack data elements requiring more than one byte of storage, since you won't be able to get more than one element in a 16-bit word. On the other hand, an array such as:

```
VAR
    MEMBLOCK : PACKED ARRAY[0..255] OF 0..255;
```

is an efficient way to represent an array of 256 bytes of memory, since two byte values (0..255) can be nicely packed into a single data word.

6

Typed Data Files

The preceding chapters have introduced you to the data structures used to
store data in a computer's memory. It's now time to present the structure
that handles more data than can be kept in the computer's memory at one
time — the data file. Before starting on this subject, here are a few words of
warning:

WARNING

The files discussed in this chapter will be files as defined in UCSD Pascal.
There are subtle, but significant, differences among some file operations in
UCSD Pascal and Standard Pascal. Many of the file operations in UCSD Pascal
are not available in Standard Pascal.

There are three kinds of files in Pascal: *typed, untyped,* and *interac-
tive.* The first two are thought of as data files in BASIC. The third kind is a
special one used for direct communication with the user through the console and keyboard. This last kind of file will be covered in the chapter on
console input and output.

Typed files are the kind used most often in maintaining information
that is stored permanently. Like other data structures, typed files must be
declared before they are used. Here are some sample file declarations:

```
MSGFILE                    : FILE OF CHAR;
TRANSFILE                  : FILE OF TRANSACTION;
NAMEFILE                   : FILE OF PERSONNAME;
```

The first of these samples, the FILE OF CHAR, is so common it actually has its own special type assigned to it by the Pascal system. The declaration TEXT is the logical equivalent to FILE OF CHAR. The other samples represent files which are groups of specific types of records. Here is one of the keys to the definition of a file . . . a file is a collection of data items—*all of the same type*—which may reside on an external medium. In the case of Pascal running on mini- or microcomputers, the external medium is usually a floppy disk. Most of the familiar BASIC file operations are available in Pascal.

Throughout this book there are examples from Applesoft BASIC, but this chapter uses examples from other dialects. This is because the file-handling routines in Applesoft are very different from those in many other versions of BASIC. Also, the Disk Operating System for the Apple was written long after the BASIC had been burned into ROM. As a result, all the disk operations in Applesoft are done through special versions of the PRINT and INPUT statements. Since most other BASICs have special statements to handle disk functions, I've picked one of them— Cromemco's 16K BASIC—to illustrate most of the examples in this chapter. Applesoft users should have little trouble following the examples, though, as most of the functions have familiar names. However, the format is somewhat different.

Creating Files

The first step in working with a data file in either BASIC or Pascal is to create the file. In many BASICs this is done as follows:

```
100 CREATE "B:PAYROLL.DATA"
```

The CREATE statement is followed by a string constant (or string variable) which becomes the file name in the diskette directory. In the Cromemco and CP/M operating systems, a single letter followed by a colon designates a particular disk drive as the destination of the file. These operating systems don't require any specification of file size or type when the file is created—the file can expand with use, threading itself through and around other files on the diskette.

UCSD Pascal places somewhat more stringent requirements when creating a data file. Of course, the first of these is defining the type of data in the file in the declaration of the file. The second requirement is knowing how long the file will be when you create it. To be sure, you can often fool the system by making a very large file and then only using part of it, but this wastes disk space and is a symptom of poor planning. The reason that you should know the size of a file is that the UCSD operating system does not dynamically allocate disk space. Data is stored on the disk in contiguous tracks and blocks (a block is 512 bytes—two sectors on most floppy disks). Other operating systems, such as Apple's DOS 3.3 or Digital Research's CPM, may use sectors from a number of different tracks—with several bytes in each sector or a part of the disk catalog pointing to the next track and sector in the file. This process of building a file from free blocks which may be located anywhere on the disk is called *dynamic allocation*. The contiguous-block method used by Pascal does not allow the use of all the disk space quite as easily, but files can be read and written somewhat faster. (Please don't confuse the method of allocation of file space with random and sequential access, which will be covered later in the chapter.)

The Pascal file is created with a REWRITE statement:

REWRITE(EMPLFILE, '#5:EMPLOYEES.DATA');

This statement creates the directory entry for the employee file on volume #5, which is normally the second disk drive. Pascal uses the word "volume" to refer to an input/output device. The volume number, or more usually a volume name, precedes the colon in the file name string. Volume names are much to be preferred, as the system will actually check the diskette in the drive to be sure of writing the data in the proper place. The REWRITE statement produces an error if it is used with a file name that already exists on the diskette.

A better way to open the employee file would be:

REWRITE (EMPLFILE, 'EMPDISK: EMPLOYEES. DATA');

This not only has the advantage of naming the specific diskette destined to receive the file, but additionally, the system searches through all the connected disk drives until it finds the one with EMPDISK. The Pascal operating system usually assigns a default volume name to the disk drives in your system. Thus, you may not have to specify the volume name when looking for a file on the default volume, but it is usually better to use a complete volume name.

The REWRITE statement creates a directory entry for the file, then prepares the system to write data to the diskette. The data will be written starting immediately after the last block used either by the system or the preceding file, or in the largest block of free space on the diskette, if there is more than one block of free space on the diskette. The data space is not actually used at this time, but any future attempts to use the space will be stopped by the operating system.

Fill 'er Up, Please!

Once a file has been created, the next step is usually to write data into it. In BASIC this is usually carried out with a series of statements:

```
100 OPEN #1,"PAYROLL.DATA"
110 FOR I = 1 TO 100
120 PUT #1, I,"NEW EMPLOYEE"
130 NEXT I
```

These statements would initialize the file with a series of dummy entries. In Pascal, the same series of operations is followed to initialize the file. Since, in Pascal, the REWRITE operation has left the file open for writing, filling it with dummy data is fairly simple:

```
FOR I: = 1 TO 100 DO
   BEGIN
      EMPLFILE∧.EMPLNUM: = I;
      EMPLFILE∧.NAME: = "NEW EMPLOYEE";
      PUT(EMPFILE);
   END; (*OF FOR LOOP*)
```

I've said it's simple, so I should explain a few of the new concepts introduced in the example. One of these I will let you take on faith for the moment — the FOR loop.

The next new concept is that of the *window variable,* a variable of the type contained in the file. It is the only component of the file accessible to the program at any time. It may help to understand the window variable if you think of a file as a long strip of microfilm. With a special magnifying glass, you can read exactly one frame of the film strip at any time. By moving the lens over the film, you can select a particular frame, which is then projected on a special screen to be read. This screen is the window variable.

When reading an item from a file, the data in one record in the file is transferred to the window variable. When writing to the file, the contents of the window variable are written to the disk.

The window variable can be treated just the same as any other variable. You can change a component of it (if it is a record variable), manipulate it with arithmetic or string operators, or set it equivalent to another variable of the same type. The window variable is designed by using the file specification (not the name in the directory, but the file designator from the declarations section) followed by the up arrow (↑). If the file is made up of complex records, the components of the record are separated from the window variable with periods, just as is the case with other records.

The second new feature of this example is the PUT statement. This one is really easy: when you PUT(EMPFILE) you simply take the data in the window variable and write it out to the disk—almost. The "almost" here means that what you really do is transfer the data into a disk buffer residing somewhere in memory. The data will stay in this buffer until one of three things happen: One, moving to another record with another PUT statement, taking you past the end of the buffer. The operating system then writes the filled buffer to the diskette, reads in the next block and continues. The second way to clear the buffer is to close the file—we'll discuss that in a page or two. In this case the buffer is also written to the diskette— at least almost always. The third, and most upsetting, way to clear the buffer is to halt or shut off the machine without closing the file. In this case, data you expected to be written to the disk never gets there. This last occurrence leads to The Rule of Closing:

THE RULE OF CLOSING

When working with important data (if it's not important, why are you bothering to put it into a file?) which is being entered from the console, open the file, write the data and close the file *after each record is entered and verified!*

Expecting that a file can be opened at the start of a program and stay successfully opened throughout the duration of a two-hour data entry session is expecting an exception to Murphy's Law. If the coffee cup falls on the reset key while the file is open, someone will have to figure out which 512-byte block is bad (there might be 20 25-byte records in the block) and correct all the entries in it. If the file is closed, someone will have to re-enter the last record, but nothing more. You can guess how easy it is to tell a frustrated clerk that 20 hastily scribbled stock transaction slips have to be entered again. You can also guess at that clerk's opinion of you, your program and the computer you suckered his boss into buying.

If you run an initialization or backup program to write a large number of records under program control, ignore the Rule of Closing; to do otherwise causes these procedures to go much more slowly than necessary. But, when starting such a procedure, tell the user what is going on so that there will be no nagging doubts that the machine has gone crazy. Unexpectedly-whirring disk drives have been known to drive even experienced programmers to the verge of insanity. The vision of hours of data entry disappearing under a maddening write head can be painfully vivid!

Since I've just discussed the PUT statement, I'll cover its companion, the GET statement, before going further. GET works much like READ in BASIC. In Pascal a GET causes the file record at the current position to be read into the window variable. After the data is transferred to the window variable, the file pointer advances to the next record. If you are already at the last record in the file, the pointer stays there and the system Boolean function EOF(FileID) becomes TRUE.

Open and Shut Cases

In the preceding rhetoric I managed to sneak another procedure by those of you who are less wary. I told you to open and close files without telling you how it should be done. Opening a file which already exists is simple and straightforward. Just use the procedure RESET instead of REWRITE.

```
RESET(EMPLFILE,'EMPDISK:EMPLOYEES.DATA');
```

opens the employee data file and sets the window variable to the first record in the file (for later reference, this is record number zero). Attempting to RESET a file which doesn't exist or is already open will result in an I/O error. Closing a file is a little more complex. The statement is simple:

```
CLOSE(PAYFILE,OPTION);
```

closes the file. It's the word OPTION that needs a little extra attention. This word can be replaced with one of the following:

> **Normal.** Closing with this option simply takes the file off line after writing out the buffer. If the file was opened with REWRITE, it will disappear from the directory. If it was opened with RESET the file remains in

the directory at its original size. No option at all is treated as a normal close.

Lock. This option does a normal close, but makes the file permanent in the directory if it was opened with REWRITE.

Purge. An option you should never let anyone but systems programmers use. It deletes files from the directory. If your application needs the file once, it will probably need it again. As far as the user is concerned, the data files should always be there. Even if the data in the file is temporary, it is probably better simply to re-write the data than to delete and re-create a file.

Crunch. This option locks the file and sets its length to extend to the last record read or written. Mistakes with this one can cause a file to shrink suddenly if you happen to close after reading a record in the middle of the file. Use this one only when initializing a file.

Standard Pascal has no facility for randomly accessing any record in a file. All files are treated as sequential and to get to a particular record, you have to start at the beginning and read forward until you get to the desired record. As a result, many programs written in standard Pascal used large data arrays to hold the contents of whole files. UCSD Pascal has added a procedure to allow positioning of the file pointer to any record in a file. This procedure is called SEEK. It is used like this:

```
SEEK(EMPLFILE,RECNUM);
```

When this procedure is called, the file pointer will be set so that the next record accessed with a GET or PUT statement will be the one pointed to by RECNUM. (The variable RECNUM would be an integer specifying a specific record—perhaps derived from an array of employee name keys.) The file designator must indicate a file which is open when the procedure is called, and the record number must be an integer or integer variable. (An implicit, but often overlooked, result of the requirement that RECNUM be an integer is that you cannot randomly access all the records in a file with more than 32767 records.)

BASIC often allows a particular record to be specified as part of the GET or PUT statement:

```
100 GET /1,RN/ A$
```

would get A$ from file number 1, record number RN. Pascal makes us separate the changing of the file pointer, with SEEK, from the reading and writing to the file. In order to read a particular record in Pascal, a sequence like this would be used:

```
SEEK(EMPLFILE,RECNUM);
GET(EMPLFILE);
```

A point to remember is that random access to a file with the SEEK command is slower than sequential access. In order to move the file pointer to a particular record, the Pascal system must multiply the record number by the length of the record, then determine exactly where that data item will be within the file. It is much quicker for the system simply to add the record length to the previous file pointer as happens with sequential access. Initializing a file with a series of statements like:

```
REWRITE(EMPLFILE,'EMPDISK:EMPLOYEES.DATA');
NEWREC.NAME: = 'NEW EMPLOYEE';
NEWREC.NUMBER: = 0;
FOR I: = 0 TO 100 DO
   BEGIN
      SEEK(EMPLFILE,I);
      EMPLFILE ∧: = NEWREC;
      PUT(EMPLFILE);
   END;
CLOSE(EMPLFILE,LOCK);
```

is a waste of time. The SEEK statement is not needed at all, since the PUT automatically advances the file pointer to the next record after writing the data to the file. The point to remember is that the SEEK function should only be used when a true random access to a file is needed. Reading or writing all the records in a file in order is certainly not *random* access!

WARNING

Two successive SEEKS without an intervening GET or PUT may leave strange garbage in the window variable and file buffer. It is also possible to SEEK past the end of a file. A GET or PUT executed at that time will cause problems. Check the value of the record number against the size of the file (as defined with a CONSTANT declaration) before the SEEK!

The End of It All

Pascal provides us with a built-in Boolean function EOF(FileID) which we can use to test whether we have reached the end of a file. This function will return a value of TRUE when you try to PUT or GET a record at the end of the file. When this happens the window variable is undefined (that means it may be filled with garbage). To those who are used to processing text files of indeterminate length, it may seem that I have devoted too little attention to the use of the EOF statement. There are two reasons for this minimal treatment.

> 1. Due to the static nature of the file allocation process in UCSD Pascal, it is important to know the size of a file before using it. This most often means filling the file with dummy information when creating it. Some element of the dummy information can be used to determine which records have been used.

> 2. Most textbooks on Pascal devote several pages to the use of the EOF function. Pick one of these—one with good example programs—and use it to investigate features such as the EOF function, which I do not cover in detail in this book.

There is another intrinsic function in UCSD Pascal, IORESULT, which allows us to test the result of any I/O operation to see whether an error occurred. The value of IORESULT will be zero if the operation proceeded normally. If an I/O error occurred, the value of the function will indicate the type of error. The system normally stops the program when an I/O error occurs. In order to be able to test IORESULT and correct errors within your program, you must disable the I/O CHECK compiler option. This is done with the statement:

(*$I-*)

which looks like a comment. The dollar sign informs the compiler that a compiler option is included inside the comment delimiters. In this case, the option tells the compiler not to produce code to automatically test the results of each I/O operation. The resulting code will run somewhat faster, but it is the responsibility of the programmer to test for successful completion of the I/O operation. Use this option with *extreme* care! There is a more complete example showing the use of the IORESULT and I- options in chapter 10.

7

The Other Kinds
of Files

Typed data files are the kind used in most business and scientific applications, but the Pascal system does allow other kinds of files and file manipulations. Untyped files are useful for bulk transfers of data. Text files can be used to store character data when sequential access is all that is needed. There are also certain special operations to carry out the most fundamental level of disk-file operations.

Untyped Files

There will be times when you will want to transfer the complete contents of one disk file to another file. When you "back up" an important data file, this is exactly what you are doing. If the file is very long, like a file with 5000 transaction records, a record-by-record transfer might take five to ten minutes. In a business or scientific environment, frequent backups are important. The more often the data is backed up, the less work will be required to restore it if a diskette should be damaged. Thus, it is in the programmer's interest to make the backup procedure fast and efficient. Untyped files, which are files with no specified type of internal structure, can be used to speed up the copying of files by a factor of five to eight.

The reason that transfers to untyped files are faster than the same operations with typed files is that the Pascal system does not have to break the untyped file down into data records. An untyped file is treated as a group of unstructured blocks, each containing 512 bytes of data. These blocks are the same unit that the operating system uses as a file buffer. The intrinsic functions BLOCKREAD and BLOCKWRITE are used to transfer complete blocks of data from an array in memory to and from disk files. The array in memory must be made up of a data type that takes up exactly one byte and should be a multiple of 512 bytes in length. Multiples of 512 bytes are necessary to maintain some sort of correspondence between a position in the array and the blocks transferred to the file. A packed array of CHAR is a handy structure for block transfers. The definitions for a good-sized data buffer might look like this:

```
TYPE
    BLOCK = PACKED ARRAY[0..511] OF CHAR;
    BUFFER = PACKED ARRAY[0..31] OF BLOCK;
VAR
    FILEBUFFER:BUFFER;
```

These declarations would reserve 16K bytes of storage as a buffer for transfers to and from untyped files. Next, declare the untyped file or files to be used in the transfer:

```
DATAFILE:FILE;
BACKUPFILE:FILE;
```

Note that, as in other declarations, both the file identifiers could have been declared on the same line, separated by commas.

Untyped data files are opened and closed with the same statements used with typed files.

```
RESET(DATAFILE,'TRDISK:TRANSACTIONS');
RESET(BACKUPFILE,'TRBACK:TRANSACTIONS');
```

As always, use volume and file names which make sense to another programmer. Note that the use of the RESET statement with the backup file assumes that the backup file has already been created and initialized on the backup disk.

The actual reading and writing are accomplished with BLOCKREAD and BLOCKWRITE:

```
INTVAL: = BLOCKREAD(DATAFILE,FILEBUFFER,NUMBLK, STARTBLK);
INTVAL: = BLOCKWRITE(BACKUPFILE,FILEBUFFER,NUMBLK,STARTBLK);
```

Since BLOCKREAD and BLOCKWRITE are functions, they return an integer value. This value is the number of blocks read or written. If a zero is returned, an error has occurred on reading or writing. Without disabled error checking, (with the (*$I – *) option, the system will halt with an error message.

The parameters used in the functions are set up as follows:

Datafile.   This is the file identifier to be used in the transfer. The file must be declared as an untyped file.

Filebuffer.   This is the packed array of characters used to store the information in memory.

Numblk.   The number of 512-byte blocks to be transferred is set by this integer.

Startblk.   This is the block number, relative to the start of the file, where the data will be read or written.

The STARTBLK variable is an optional parameter. If it is not used, transfers start at the beginning of the file (block zero). It is also possible to start the transfer from a point inside the array by specifying an index. Of course, you can substitute your own variable names into the parameter block.

Text Files

A text file contains only ASCII characters. In fact, the following Pascal declarations are equivalent:

```
MESSAGES = TEXT;
MESSAGES = FILE OF CHAR;
```

A text file can store anything from a single line message to the complete source code for a large compiler. In fact, text files are quite often used by programs like compilers and assemblers which use this type of file to store the source code to be processed. Because many college students use Pascal to write editors, assemblers and compilers, most textbooks contain very thorough explanations and lots of examples of this type of file. Text files are less often used in business and scientific programs where the data is more structured. The unit of information read from a text file can be either a single character or a complete line of characters terminated by a carriage return character.

Since the lines of characters in a text file may vary in length (generally from one to 80 characters), these files can be an effective way to store certain types of data such as messages, letters or reminders. The disadvantage of having lines of variable length is that you must read or write the file sequentially from the start, since jumping into the middle of the file will probably put you somewhere in the middle of a line.

Pascal provides the intrinsic procedures READLN and WRITELN for use with text files. The READLN procedure will read data from a text file until it encounters a carriage return. The procedure is capable of translating character strings encountered into real or integer numbers. This capability is shown in the following example:

```
VAR
   INFILE:TEXT ;
   INTNUM:INTEGER:
   REALNUM:REAL;

BEGIN
   RESET(INFILE,'TEMPFILE.TEXT' ');
   READLN(INFILE,INTNUM,REALNUM);
END;
```

Here the input file is opened and one integer and one real value are read from the file. The character strings which represent the numbers must be separated by a space. Characters other than spaces, digits or decimal points in real numbers will cause an input/output error. With the exception of the special non-disk files like the console and the printer, text files are generally not a good place either to look for or send numbers. In a business application program, the best use for text files is as a place to store string data such as messages or reminders temporarily.

In UCSD Pascal, console files are selected by default when there is no file specified as the first parameter for either READLN or WRITELN.

```
READLN(NAMESTRING);
```

would read a string from the keyboard (while echoing it to the screen).

If this discussion of text files seems rather brief in comparison to other books on Pascal, rest assured it is only because *I* have found them less useful than typed data files in programs I have written. Other programmers may use text files much more extensively. The use of the console, printer and other non-disk files will be covered in later chapters.

Direct Device Management

UCSD Pascal allows you to talk directly to I/O devices with two procedures, UNITREAD and UNITWRITE. These procedures bypass the catalog which keeps track of the files on a disk and can directly access any block on the diskette. For other I/O devices such as printers and MODEMS (devices for transmitting and receiving data over telephone lines) this capability for direct access does not have such important implications. However, the fact that UNITREAD and UNITWRITE allows you to work with any block on the diskette gives you power that must not be abused. If improperly used, these intrinsic procedures can result in scrambled catalogs and lost data.

REMINDER

UNITREAD and UNITWRITE are *procedures* and do not return an integer value, while BLOCKREAD and BLOCKWRITE are *functions* and return a value.

The UNITREAD and UNITWRITE procedures operate directly on devices specified by I/O device number. This device number is an integer which specifies exactly which I/O interface will be used for the transfer. The device numbers used on the Apple II are:

#1: CONSOLE:	The CRT screen and keyboard with echo	
#2: KEYBOARD:	Keyboard input with no echo	
#4: (VOL NAME):	First disk drive (boot disk)	
#5: (VOL NAME):	Second disk drive	
#6: PRINTER:	Line printer (either serial or parallel)	
#7: REMIN:	Remote Input (serial card or modem, which may be used as an external terminal)	
#8: REMOUT:	Remote Output (serial card or modem— same device as #7)	
#9-#12	More disk drives.	

The UNITREAD procedure would be called like this:

UNITREAD (DEVNUM,DATABUFFER,BLEN,BLKNUM,ITYPE)

The DEVNUM parameter is an integer—note that if you use an in-line constant, you do not use the '#' before the ':' after the number. The data will be read into the buffer variable specified in the second parameter. This variable should be a packed array of bytes or characters. If the device is blocked-structured (that is, a disk drive), the array should be a multiple of 512 bytes. An array of blocks as shown with the BLOCKREAD example is a good structure to use with disk drives. The BLEN parameter defines the number of bytes to be transferred. Note that it is not necessary to transfer complete blocks of data with these procedures. The blocknumber parameter is optional and is used only with disk drives, and specifies the block where the transfer is to begin. The default value is zero.

WARNING

Remember that blocks zero to six of a diskette are the bootstrap and directory blocks. You should write to these blocks only if you are *very* sure of the effect of your operations.

The last parameter ITYPE specifies the type of transfer to take place. A zero specifies a synchronous transfer, and a one specifies an asynchronous transfer. For disk transfers, leave this a zero. Zero is the default value, and the parameter is optional in any case. With the types of I/O devices used on most microcomputers, this parameter probably has little effect.

A third unit-oriented procedure, UNITCLEAR, can be used to reset any I/O device to its power-up state. This might be useful if a modem or serial device might have been left in some special state by a previous operation or error condition. This procedure also cancels any pending input or output for the device.

The UNITCLEAR procedure can be used to check whether a particular I/O device is plugged into the computer. This is done by disabling the I/O error checking, then attempting to clear the device. If the device is plugged in and operating, an IORESULT of zero will be returned. A non-zero value of IORESULT indicates that the device is not available for use.

There are two other unit I/O intrinsics defined in UCSD Pascal, UNITBUSY and UNITWAIT. These intrinsics test the status of the I/O device and are designed for systems where the I/O devices are interrupt-driven. If you are running Pascal on a minicomputer, particularly a time-shared system, consult your reference manuals for more information on these procedures. Since the I/O on most microcomputers does not use interrupts, I won't discuss these any further.

8

Console and Printer Input and Output

Effective communication between the computer program and the user, through the console, is just as important as efficient data structures. The ability to translate information on the console screen to a printed record is also necessary in a business environment. Every good business program written in BASIC is testimony to these statements. A BASIC program with only rudimentary data structures can be widely and effectively used simply because it communicates efficiently with its users. The programmer's struggle to cope with the limited data structures of BASIC is completely hidden from the user. On the other hand, an elegantly structured program won't win many users with input statements that ask questions like, "D1, R1,S1?".

Ask and Ye Shall Receive

Since every request for input from the console should be accompanied by an effective prompt for the proper type of input, we'll look first at output statements—which you have to use for the prompts in Pascal. Pascal does not allow mixing input and output in a single statement, as is possible in BASIC with a statement like:

```
100   INPUT "WHAT IS YOUR NAME? ",N$
```

With Pascal we have to do the prompting with a WRITE statement before requesting the input.

The WRITE statement works much like the PRINT statement in BASIC. You can write the value of one or more variables on the console in an unformatted manner with a simple statement like:

```
WRITE(HEIGHT,WEIGHT);
```

The values to be written are grouped inside the parentheses and are separated by commas. When WRITE statement is finished, the cursor of the console will be positioned after the last written value. This is equivalent to the BASIC statement:

```
100   PRINT HT;WT;
```

Thus, the WRITE statement functions like a PRINT statement where the terminating semicolon instructs the computer not to move to the next line of output. The WRITELN statement also prints the values of the variables, but then moves the cursor to the next line on the screen or terminal. This is equivalent to the BASIC PRINT statement without the terminating semicolon. Each of the variables written with the WRITE statement will be printed directly after the previous one. The standard Pascal on some large computers often writes numeric variables in a field of fixed size—which may vary with different computers. UCSD Pascal does insert a single space before the first digit in a positive real value, but this space will be used by the minus sign if the number is negative. If we execute the following series of statements:

```
VAR
    A,B :INTEGER;
    C   :REAL;
```

```
BEGIN
    A : = 1;
    B : = 23;
    C : = 4;

    WRITELN(A,B,C);
END;
```

we would get the following output:

```
123   4.00000
```

The 1 and the 23 have been run together, but the 4 is separated by the space that is reserved for the sign of the real variable. Note also that, in an unformatted write statement, UCSD Pascal defaults to scientific format for real variables. Thus, a value of 789 would be printed as 7.89000E2 and a value of .0034 would be written as 3.40000E-3. These conventions lead to another rule:

THE WRITER'S RULE

If you write more than one value on a line, be explicit about numeric formatting. Use unformatted **WRITE** statements only when there is no possibility of confusion.

Explicit Numeric Formatting

Explicit numeric formatting is accomplished in Pascal by appending a *minimum field width designator* to the variable name inside the WRITE statement. This field width parameter is separated from the variable name with a colon. When the field width is specified, the compiler causes the program to use at least the designated number of columns to write the number. The value will be right-justified with enough spaces inserted before the number to fill the field. If the number is too big, it will extend past the right end of the field. Numbers which turn out to be larger than anticipated are, thus, an easy way to mess up a nicely formatted table or report.

If we use the same numbers as before (1, 23 and 4.0) but write them with the following statement:

        WRITE(A:2,B:4,C:8);

we would get the following output:

        b1bb23b4.00000

where the "b" would show up as a space in an actual display. I used the "b" to make it easier to count the spaces. When writing real numbers, we are allowed to add a second colon and a field specifier which will determine the number of digits to be printed after the decimal point. If we wrote the values of A, B and C like this:

        WRITE(A:2,B:4,C:8:2);

we would get output like this:

        b1bb23bbbb4.00

The value for C still uses a total of eight columns, but the number is displayed with two digits after the decimal point. If the value of C was 4.386 then the output would look like:

        b1bb23bbbb4.39

As you can see, the value of C has been *rounded* to two decimal places.

    String variables can also be printed with explicit formatting in Pascal. The string variable name is simply followed by a colon and the field width designator. The output string will be right-justified inside the field.

    These explicit formats for numeric output are much akin to the PRINT USING statement available in some BASIC interpreters. We could get the same type of output format from BASIC using this statement:

        100 PRINT USING "## #### #####.##",A%,B%,C

Since the details of the PRINT USING statement vary quite a bit from BASIC to BASIC, I won't go into any further detail here. If you've been using a BASIC without a PRINT USING facility, such as Applesoft, you should really appreciate the formatted output capability of Pascal. Programmers have been known to discuss for hours the best way to format numbers into neat columns with Applesoft. I'm not sure any two of them have agreed on the best method, even after years of effort.

Caution! Strings Attached!

We have all used string constants in our BASIC PRINT statements to explain exactly what we are printing. Statements like:

100 PRINT "THE VALUE OF X IS ";X

are used to show results on the screen with explanatory text. Pascal allows us to do much the same thing by including a string constant inside a WRITE statement. In Pascal, however, the string constant is defined by single quotation marks (') or apostrophes. The equivalent to the BASIC statement above would be:

WRITELN('THE VALUE OF X IS ',X);

If you need to print an apostrophe in the output, simply use two of them in a row in the string constant. The statement

WRITELN('YOU DON''T HAVE TO STRUGGLE WITH ''S');

would produce

YOU DON'T HAVE TO STRUGGLE WITH 'S

This is much simpler than the contortions necessary in some versions of BASIC to print a quotation mark.

When you are using UCSD Pascal with a CRT-type terminal (or a video display machine like the Apple) there are several special control characters and commands which allow you to modify the display:

```
PAGE(OUTPUT);           (*move cursor to upper left and*)
                        (*clear screen—like HOME in Applesoft*)

WRITE(CHR(29));         (*clear from cursor to end of*)
                        (*current line*)

WRITE(CHR(11));         (*clear from cursor to end of*)
                        (*screen*)

GOTOXY (XCOL,YLINE);    (*move cursor directly to column XCOL*)
                        (*and line YLINE.    XCOL can*)
                        (*range from 0 to 79    and YLINE*)
                        (*may range from 0 to 23*)
```

The specific ASCII character used for some of the functions may vary from system to system. The Pascal operating system generally provides a utility program which allows you to define the ASCII character used for each function. Of course, if you are using an external terminal, it must be capable of executing direct cursor control commands to use the GOTOXY command. The actual strings sent to the terminal for direct cursor control vary from terminal to terminal. The UCSD Pascal Manual discusses these differences and contains instructions for the modification of the Pascal system to work properly with a number of popular terminals.

An often-used feature of BASIC which is missing in Pascal is the TAB command. However, we can simulate many of the functions of the TAB command with formatted output in Pascal. The BASIC line

```
100 PRINT(TAB(10);X;TAB(20);Y;TAB(30);H)
```

would be transformed into

```
WRITELN(X:10:2,Y:10:2,HEIGHT:10:2);
```

where the minimum field width is used to space out the numbers. Note that the TAB function prints the numbers after the specified column, while the Pascal version ensures that decimal points will be aligned and trailing zeroes added to make a nice-looking table. Of course, you could get the same results in BASIC with a PRINT USING statement. It is possible to write a TAB function in Pascal to allow you to emulate the BASIC TAB function directly, but I've found that the combination of the GOTOXY and formatted print commands are all that is needed to produce nicely-formatted output on the CRT.

Console Input: 53 Keys to Success

Now that we can ask the operator to feed the computer, we will see just how to get the data into a Pascal program. The most-used procedure for getting input from the console is READLN (short for Read a Line). That is, input will be accepted until an End-of-Line character (a carriage return) is encountered. READLN is very close to the BASIC INPUT statement, but there are a few subtle differences. The statements:

```
100 INPUT "ENTER VALUE FOR A: ";A
```

and

```
WRITE('ENTER VALUE FOR A: ');
READLN(A);
```

are equivalent in that both will accept a series of digits followed by a carriage return and assign the number to the variable A. The BASIC INPUT statement, however, is more forgiving and will give you a message like ??RE-ENTER: if you happen to enter a series of non-numeric characters like "Sam." The Pascal READLN procedure terminates your program with a fatal error given the same input. There are ways to check the Pascal version for proper input, and we'll go through those when discussing special input routines. For the moment, simply remember that Pascal is somewhat picky about the data entered in response to a READLN statement.

Pascal also allows you to enter several values, each to be assigned to a different variable. The statements:

```
WRITE('ENTER A, B, AND C: ');
READLN(A,B,C);
```

are just as valid as:

```
100 INPUT "ENTER A, B, AND C:";A,B,C
```

but there is one very large difference in how the numbers should be entered. Pascal does not allow you to enter commas to separate the numbers, while BASIC must have them! In Pascal the commas will cause a fatal error; you must separate the numbers with spaces. Many versions of BASIC completely ignore the spaces and run all the numbers together if you try to enter three numbers without commas between them. This all leads to yet another rule:

THE RULE OF READLN

When using READLN, always prompt for each number separately and only accept one value at a time. If someone other than yourself will use the program, use an error-checking input routine to screen for potentially fatal errors.

If you follow this rule, people who use your programs will thank you. Input statements which asked the user for six variables, all separated by commas, were perhaps more practical when the console was a hard-copy terminal printing at 10 characters per second. In an era when most consoles are CRT terminals operating at 30 to 960 characters per second, it makes much more sense to ask for each variable with a specific prompt. The proper use of the GOTOXY procedure and sensible prompt statements can make entering even the most complex data as simple as filling out a well-designed form with a pencil that erases perfectly.

Pascal has another data entry procedure which is really a subsection of the READLN procedure. This is the READ procedure. The READ procedure does not read until a carriage return, but simply keeps reading until it has filled up all the variables, or until you break out of the loop which includes the READ statement. When used with CHAR variables, this procedure is somewhat similar to the GET statement available in some forms of BASIC. When the READ procedure is called, it sets two system Boolean variables, EOLN and EOF, if it received either a carriage return or an EOF character, respectively.

One time when the READ procedure is very useful is when you simply want a single character response to a menu on the screen. The procedure is used like this:

```
WRITELN('Which program would you like?');
WRITELN('A : Enter new client data.');
WRITELN('B : Review client transactions.');
WRITELN('C : Print mailing labels.');
WRITELN;
WRITELN('Enter your choice by letter: ');
READ(ACHAR);
```

The program would then activate one of the menu selections based on the keyboard entry. The READ procedure is also useful as part of a procedure which reads a sequence of characters, carefully checks each one for validity (which may vary with the particular application), and builds up an output string.

Putting It Down on Paper

There will always come a time when you need to transfer the information on your video screen to a piece of paper, if only so you can find a more comfortable chair in which to lean back, relax and consider the information the computer has prepared. Pascal allows you to use the WRITE and WRITELN statements with a device other than the console by specifying the device as a parameter in the statement:

WRITELN(PRINT1,'THIS WILL BE PRINTED');

This statement would write the statement in single quotation marks to the output device PRINT1. This is a lot like using a printer in BASIC where a line like:

100 PRINT #1, "THIS WILL BE PRINTED"

sends the output to device #1. Many forms of BASIC consider the printer to be a special form of output file, as does Pascal.

Pascal considers output devices to be a form of text file, so you must open the file properly before you can write to it. This means that you must declare the file as a variable:

VAR
    PRINT1:TEXT;

The declaration of the printer should be a global declaration, since all procedures in the program will have to share a single printer.

The printer is activated by associating the file designator (PRINT1) with the actual device in a REWRITE statement:

REWRITE(PRINT1,'PRINTER:');

The actual device PRINTER: (with a colon after the name) is a volume name reserved by the Pascal system for a printer. In the Apple system, this printer must be driven by an interface card plugged into I/O slot ÷1 in the back of the Apple. Other systems generally have a system configuration program which defines the type and location of the printer interface for the operating system.

Once the print device has been activated, you may write to it just as you would to the console (except that you cannot use direct cursor addressing—the GOTOXY procedure). All the methods of formatting are just as important with printed output as they are for console output. In fact, good formatting with printed records may be more important, since it may be seen by more people than the console displays.

Once you have finished with the printer, close it like any other file. In the case of a printer, you will not lose printed records if the file is improperly closed, but why allow an exception that could get to be a bad habit? A printer is closed like any other device:

```
CLOSE(PRINT1);
```

There will often be times when you would like to choose whether information should be routed to the console or to the printer. This can be done by considering the console as a device which must be explicitly activated, rather than allowing it to be the default device as is usually the case. Start with a declaration of the file designator for the device:

```
VAR
   OUTDEV:TEXT;
```

Then pick either the console or the printer as the output device by executing *one* of the following statements:

```
REWRITE(OUTDEV,'CONSOLE:');
```

or

```
REWRITE(OUTDEV,'PRINTER:');
```

After the device is opened, all output directed to OUTDEV goes to the selected device. Any WRITE statement without the OUTDEV parameter still goes to the console by default. The type of statement you would use to decide between the two devices is covered in the next chapter on control statements.

9

Control Structures

When you get right down to the nitty-gritty, any computer program can be broken down into four parts:

1. Get some data from the keyboard, an existing file, or even from statements in the program itself.

2. Manipulate the data in some way.

3. Do something with the results—save them in a file or show them to the user.

4. If it's not time to go home, go back to part 1.

The amount of time and effort expended on each of these parts can vary considerably from program to program. A complex engineering program may ask the user for ten numbers, then spend a minute or two in step two. The output may be as simple as one or two numbers—numbers that tell the engineer to use the next larger size I-beam in the bridge supports. On the other hand, many business and accounting programs spend about 95 percent of their time in steps one and three. Unless you are a very creative accountant (a professional inclination frowned upon by law, the IRS and the firm's stockholders), you probably spend very little time manipulating financial data. Most of your (or your program's) time will be spent collecting and verifying data, then displaying it in tables or reports.

Up to this point, I've described how steps one and three work in Pascal; I have said very little about step two. This is, in part, because I didn't really feel it was necessary to tell you that Pascal can add, subtract, multiply and divide. Since this book isn't intended to be an exhaustive reference manual on the Pascal language, I've left out the descriptions of mathematical operators that work exactly the same way in Pascal as they do in BASIC. The differences between Pascal and BASIC lie primarily in their data structures and the way the languages control the sequence of program steps. The second difference, which is item number four in the list, is the subject of this chapter.

Only the simplest of programs, like determining the mean of three numbers just to show it can be done, execute a set of program steps just once, then stop. For most of us, a great part of the power of a computer lies in its ability to carry out the same series of steps over and over, without getting bored or making arithmetic errors before that first cup of coffee. The program structures for controlling repetitive actions are available in Pascal, as they must be in any computer language. Some of them are so close to their counterparts in BASIC that you won't be able to detect the difference. Others have no equivalents in BASIC and you have been simulating them with groups of statements for years. If you've written any complex programs, you have used the logical equivalents of the Pascal control structures dozens of times. But, in BASIC, you have had to use combinations of IFs, GOTOs and ON X GOSUB to achieve the effect of a single statement in Pascal.

FOR Loops

To ease into the subject of control structures gently, let's start with an old and familiar friend. One of the first things any budding programmer does when he gets his hands on a computer is to write a program like:

```
10 FOR I = 1 TO 1000
20 PRINT I
30 NEXT I
```

Then you type RUN and sit back with a foolish grin and a feeling of pride watching a thousand completely useless numbers flicker across the screen. There is such an elemental rush of power in being able to do something a hundred or a thousand times at the touch of a key, that the FOR loop may be the most demonstrated feature of any computer language. This is particularly so in BASIC where you can write and run a program so quickly. Fear not, for Pascal also has FOR loops. Unfortunately, you won't be able to use them to impress friends quite so easily because of the time required to write, compile and run the program. The FOR loop in Pascal starts out just like its counterpart in BASIC:

```
FOR I: = 1 TO 1000 DO
```

Notice that there's no terminating semicolon after the DO. That's because the statement isn't finished yet. You have to DO something!

```
FOR I: =  1 TO 1000 DO WRITELN(I);
```

Now we have finished the statement by DOing something—writing the value of I to the console. The FOR loop can also be written so that the control variable (I) is decremented rather than incremented. This is accomplished by using DOWNTO instead of TO.

```
FOR I: = 1000 DOWNTO 1 DO WRITELN(I);
```

would start at 1000 and count backwards. Perhaps it's a sign of my determination always to move forward, but I can't remember having used DOWNTO at all in the last year.

If the FOR loop could only execute a single action after the DO, its usefulness would be severely limited. But, of course, it isn't that limited. The statement to be executed may be a compound statement bracketed by the BEGIN . . . END pair. A more complex loop might look like this:

```
FOR SENATORS : = 1 TO 100 DO
   BEGIN
      WRITE('SENATOR''S NAME: ');
      READLN(NAME);
      WRITELN(PRINTER,'Dear Senator ',NAME);
      . . .
      . . .
      (* PRINT TEXT OF PROTEST AGAINST PROPOSED TAX *)
      (* ON COMPUTER SOFTWARE *)
      . . .
      . . .
   END;
```

As a matter of fact, this loop is probably a little too complex. The same rule applies in Pascal that you have probably read time after time in BASIC manuals: Never start a FOR loop you don't intend to finish. In Pascal there are other control structures explicitly designed to allow a change of mind, exiting the loop at will. If you start a FOR loop, let it run until it's finished. My own preference is to use this loop structure only in those situations where the computer can carry out its actions without human intervention. When requesting input from the keyboard, use a loop structure that allows a graceful exit at coffee break time. There are a few important points to remember when using the FOR loop in Pascal.

1. The control variable (I in the first example) should not be changed by an assignment statement inside the loop. The starting and ending values, if they are variables, should also remain inviolate until the loop is finished.

2. The control variable, the starting value and the ending value must all be of the same type. The variables may be integers, scalars or subranges. Real variables are not allowed. The statement

```
FOR RNUM : = 1.5 TO 2.5 DO
```

is illegal in Pascal. If you need to work with fractions in a loop, you will have to calculate them inside the loop.

3. The control variable always increments (or decrements if DOWNTO is used) by one. There is no equivalent to the STEP facility in BASIC.

4. If the starting value is less than the ending value, the DO statement never gets executed, because the value is tested against the limits before the DO statement. Many versions of BASIC always execute the statements inside a loop at least once because the test is made after the statements are executed.

Repeat . . . Until Loops,

The REPEAT statement causes a Pascal statement to be executed over and over again until the condition specified after UNTIL is satisfied. To achieve the same results as we did with our FOR loop example, we would write:

```
I: = 1;
REPEAT
    WRITELN(I);
    I: = I + 1;
UNTIL I = 1000;
```

This series of statements looks much like a series you might see in BASIC:

```
100 I = 1
110 PRINT I
120 I = I + 1
130 IF I = 1000 THEN GOTO 150
140 GOTO 110
150 REM EXIT LOOP HERE
```

As you can see, the Pascal statements are somewhat less complex. Of course, I could have written the series of BASIC statements more compactly by using

```
130 IF I<1000 THEN GOTO 110
```

but I chose to use exactly the same test for loop termination in the two examples. The REPEAT . . . UNTIL series always executes the included statements at least once, since the test for termination is made after the statements are executed the first time. The series terminates when the Boolean variable or expression following the UNTIL becomes true. Unlike the FOR loop this series of expressions can be interrupted at any time with any test or condition that alters the tested variable or expression.

A quite common use of the REPEAT . . . UNTIL sequence is in displaying a sequence of records on the console while allowing the operator to terminate the sequence at any time. A program segment to display a series of names and telephone numbers would look like this:

```
RECNUM: = 1;
ENDUP: = FALSE;
REPEAT
    WRITE(PERSREC[RECNUM].NAME:20);
    WRITELN(PERSREC[RECNUM].PHONE:10);
    RECNUM: = RECNUM + 1;
    IF RECNUM = LASTNAME THEN ENDUP: = TRUE;
    IF KEYPRESSED THEN ENDUP: = TRUE;
UNTIL ENDUP = TRUE;
```

There are two separate tests made, either of which may set the Boolean variable ENDUP to TRUE and terminate the loop. The first simply checks to see whether all the data have been displayed. The second calls a function which tests the keyboard to see if any key has been pressed. Depending on how this function works with a particular computer, you may or may not have to read the keyboard to reset the character-available flag. When you have more than one test occurring, it is easier to follow if you split them up rather than group them all into one large Boolean expression after the UNTIL.

WHILE. . .DO Sequence

The third looping structure in Pascal, the WHILE. . .DO sequence, is much like the REPEAT. . .UNTIL structure. The difference is that when WHILE is used, the test for termination is made before the statements are executed. If the example above were written with this structure it would look like this:

```
RECNUM: = 1;
ENDUP: = FALSE;
WHILE NOT ENDUP DO
BEGIN
    WRITE(PERSREC[RECNUM].NAME:20);
    WRITELN(PERSREC[RECNUM].PHONE:10);
    RECNUM: = RECNUM + 1;
    IF RECNUM = LASTNAME THEN ENDUP: = TRUE;
    IF KEYPRESSED THEN ENDUP: = TRUE;
END;   (* OF WHILE NOT ENDUP *)
```

There are several important differences in the way this loop performs. The first is that the loop executes while the test condition is true. The REPEAT loop executes UNTIL the test condition is true. Thus we have to use the NOT statement to negate the Boolean variable in the test. A second, and not so obvious, difference is that, if allowed to run without interruption, the WHILE loop will display one less record than the REPEAT loop. This is because the last record will not get displayed at all. The value of ENDUP will become true after the next-to-last record is displayed and the loop will terminate before displaying the last record. You could display the last record by simply moving the IF RECNUM = LASTNAME. . . statement to a position just before RECNUM: = RECNUM + 1. In this case the value would be tested after the display of the last record. This is just one demonstration of the ways in which the ordering of statements, particularly when testing for loop termination, can alter the results of your program.

IF Not Bored, Then Keep Reading

The next program-control statement we will examine is an old friend. In fact, you have seen it in the examples of the loop constructs and probably taken it for granted. The IF. . .THEN structure looks so much like its counterpart in BASIC, I'm sure you had no trouble understanding its function. It's time for a more formal introduction. The IF statement allows you to decide whether a statement (simple or complex) will be executed, based on the value of a Boolean variable or expression. We saw it used this way when testing the value of the record number in the examples of loop constructs:

```
IF RECNUM = LASTNAME THEN ENDUP: = TRUE;
```

The IF statement can be controlled by a full range of Boolean expressions. The numeric (and string) comparisons $=$, $>$, $<$, $>=$, $<=$, $<>$ function in Pascal just as they do in BASIC, so I'm not saying anything more about them. The IF statement can also accept a Boolean variable for the control variable.

```
IF ENDUP THEN WRITELN('ALL RECORDS DISPLAYED.');
```

This statement will tell you when all the records have been displayed if it is added to the end of the display loop in one of the sample loop structures. If this statement is executed when ENDUP is false, the program simply continues to the next statement.

Pascal also allows statements of the form IF. . . .THEN Statement1 ELSE Statement2. With this form, you choose between two alternatives based on the Boolean expression. If the expression is true, then the statement after THEN is executed. If the expression is false, the statement after ELSE will be executed. There are a few details about this form of the structure that deserve an example:

```
IF RECNUM < MAXREC THEN
    BEGIN
        SPACELEFT: = MAXREC – RECNUM;
        WRITELN('THERE IS ROOM FOR',SPACELEFT,'MORE RECORDS);
    END
ELSE   WRITELN('NO MORE ROOM IN DIRECTORY FILE');
```

As you can see, it is possible to have a number of statements (with a BEGIN . . . END pair) be executed by the IF . . . THEN statement. An important point to note is that there is no semicolon at the end of the compound statement before the ELSE part of the IF . . . THEN . . . ELSE structure. In fact, putting the automatic semicolon here, as you would after almost every other occurrence of END, will generate a compiler error. That semicolon tricks the compiler into thinking that the statement was just an IF . . . THEN sequence, and it is left with an unconnected ELSE.

CASE Statements

The IF . . . THEN . . . ELSE structure provides a way to control program flow when there are just two possible outcomes. Quite often, though, there are decisions to be made where there are more than two possible choices. BASIC provides a rudimentary facility for handling these choices with the ON X GOSUB (or GOTO) structure. To write out the names of the days of the week we might write a program like this:

```
100 INPUT "WHICH DAY OF THE WEEK (1-7)"; W1
110 PRINT "THAT IS ";
120 ON W1 GOSUB 210,220,230,240,250,260,270
130 STOP
200 REM PRINT ONE OF THE WEEKDAYS
210 PRINT "SUNDAY":RETURN
220 PRINT "MONDAY":RETURN
230 PRINT "TUESDAY":RETURN
240 PRINT "WEDNESDAY":RETURN
250 PRINT "THURSDAY":RETURN
260 PRINT "FRIDAY":RETURN
270 PRINT "SATURDAY":RETURN
```

This program works as long as you enter a number between one and seven. Most versions of BASIC simply continue to statement 130 if a number greater than seven is entered. Some versions produce a run-time error if a negative number is entered. The point here is that when using this type of decision-making step, always be sure that you are testing a value which is reasonable. Some form of input error checking would be necessary if this was part of a package of business programs.

Pascal has a facility for making multiple-way decisions which is much like the BASIC ON. . .GOSUB. It is the CASE EXPRESSION OF statement and it looks like this:

```
CASE DAYNUM OF
   1:WRITELN('SUNDAY');
   2:WRITELN('MONDAY');
   3:WRITELN('TUESDAY');
   4:WRITELN('WEDNESDAY');
   5:WRITELN('THURSDAY');
   6:WRITELN('FRIDAY');
   7:WRITELN('SATURDAY');
  END;   (*CASE DAYNUM OF...*)
```

The statement begins with the word CASE followed by an expression which must be a scalar type with a finite range of values. This means that the expression cannot have a real value or be a Boolean expression. Integer, subrange, scalar and CHAR types may be used with the CASE statement. The expression is followed by the word OF, then a list of possible choices. Each choice starts with a constant value to be matched followed by a colon. Any executable statement, including compound statements, follows the colon. If the expression matches the constant, the statement is executed. If none of the constants matches the expression, then UCSD Pascal continues with the next program statement—much like BASIC. Standard Pascal generates an error if no match is found.

A very common way to use the CASE statement is in making selections from a menu:

```
REPEAT
   WRITELN('WHICH PROGRAM DO YOU WANT?');
   (* SELECTIONS SPACED OVER TO INDENT THEM UNDER QUESTION *)
   WRITELN('    A: ACCOUNTS PAYABLE');
   WRITELN('    B: ACCOUNTS RECEIVABLE');
   WRITELN('    C: GENERAL LEDGER');
   WRITELN('    D: TERMINATE PROGRAM');
   WRITELN;
   WRITE('ENTER YOUR CHOICE BY LETTER:   ');
   WRITE(CHR(7));
   READ(KEYBOARD, SELECTION);
  UNTIL SELECTION IN ['A'..'D'];
  (* NOW WE HAVE A VALID SELECTION *)
```

```
CASE SELECTION OF
  'A':PAYABLES;
  'B':RCVABLES;
  'C':LEDGER;
  'D':CLOSEFILES;
END;    (* CASE SELECTION OF... *)
```

This program segment displays a menu, then prompts for and accepts a single character of input. If the character is not a valid input (it is not in the set of characters A through D), the menu is written again. Each time the menu is written, a bell (CHR(7)) is beeped on the terminal to notify the user that the program is waiting for input. If the input character is a valid selection, then the program proceeds to the CASE statement. There, the program decides if one of the three procedures (which may be full-fledged programs in themselves will be activated. If selection D was picked, the program executes a procedure to close the files, then continues with the statement after the CASE statement which would gracefully terminate the program.

GOTO: The Last Resort

There is one last control statement allowed in Pascal. It is the statement most often used by BASIC programmers: the GOTO statement. It is used in much the same way in Pascal as it is in BASIC:

```
If X>100 THEN GOTO 100;
```

This is a perfectly valid Pascal statement. Since Pascal does not use line numbers, the label 100 must be defined at the very beginning of the program . . . right after the program name and before any declared constants or variables:

```
PROGRAM TEST;

LABEL 100;

CONST MAXNAME = 1000;
VAR X:INTEGER;
. . . .

. . . .
BEGIN
    . . . .

    IF X >MAXNAME THEN GOTO 100
    . . . .

    . . . .
    100: WRITELN('X IS TOO LARGE')
    (* NOW END THE PROGRAM *)
```

The use of the GOTO statement in Pascal is strongly discouraged in almost every book I've read on the language. This is because the GOTO can cause you to skip large portions of the code in a program. Unnecessary use of GOTO can make following a program extremely difficult. I'll discuss this more when we get to the discussion of structured programming in chapter 10. For now, I'll just say I haven't found any situation yet where it was absolutely necessary to use a GOTO. With careful thought, the other program control statements of Pascal should be sufficient and will help keep your programs more readable.

There are a number of restrictions on exactly where you can GO TO in a program. Generally you cannot go to a label outside the procedure in which it is called. It is also illegal to jump into the middle of a more deeply nested procedure or compound statement. Because of the confusion it may cause, UCSD Pascal explicitly discourages the use of GOTO by having a compiler option which will not allow the use of the statement at all.

10

More on
Program Structure

If you have read straight through the book to this point, you have learned enough about Pascal to start writing your own programs. Before you get started on any really large projects, I'd like to say a little about program structure and how it affects the process of writing programs. The applications programs you write will be designed to accept certain items of data, manipulate and store the data, then tell the user something about that data, either immediately or some time later. Before writing the program, have a clear idea of its goals: what do you want the computer to accomplish?

You Should Talk to My Analyst!

Deciding exactly what the computer should accomplish, what system resources will be needed, and the limitations of the resulting system are the job of the *systems analyst*. The systems analyst talks to the prospective users of the computer and finds out exactly what is expected. If the user is working with a limited budget (of both time and money), the analyst must acquaint the user with the hard facts of the computer world. It isn't always easy to tell a customer that you can't get the same performance from a $5000 microcomputer that you can from a $500,000 minicomputer or small mainframe. Quite often in the case of the small programming business, the systems analyst and the programmer are the same person. This can be both an advantage and a disadvantage. It certainly helps the programmer to understand the customer's desires. On the other hand, many small points may never be written down on the assumption that all the details of the customer's requirements will be perfectly remembered when it comes time to write the program.

A systems analyst listening to the representative of a brokerage house might end up with a set of program specifications in the following manner:

Customer: I want a computer to help me keep track of my clients and their transactions.

Systems Analyst: Simple data base management problem.

Customer: I have about 350 clients. I need to know their names, addresses, telephone numbers and when I last contacted them.

Systems Analyst: Set file size at 500 client name and personal data records. If the computer is successful in helping the customer, he will probably add to his client list.

Customer: Some of my clients only have one or two transactions per year. Others have 60 or 70 transactions per year. The average is about six or seven transactions per client.

Systems Analyst: Maybe a linked list file structure to use file space efficiently with varying numbers of transactions for each client.

Customer: I need to know what stocks a client has bought or sold, when the transaction occurred, and the dollar amounts involved.

Systems Analyst: I'd better make sure to ask him about the exact nature of a transaction record later on.

Customer: Sometimes I want to send out mailings to all clients in certain categories, or to everyone who holds a certain stock.

Systems Analyst: Oh-oh! Add category variable to client record. Add module to search for holders of a given stock. This means that each transaction must have a pointer to the owner of the stock. Add line printer with forms tractor to hardware list.

Customer: You know, it would really be nice if I could update the value of the client's portfolios by having the computer connect directly to the Dow Jones wire.

Systems Analyst: Add communications port and MODEM to hardware list. What are the protocols for communications with Dow Jones? Define storage space for current price as well as purchase price for each transaction.

Customer: And maybe the computer could even dial the phone when I want to talk to a certain client when I'm reviewing a portfolio.

Systems Analyst: What does he mean by "reviewing a portfolio"? Make sure communications interface has auto-dial capability. Maybe I should go back to writing computer games.

Customer: Can I get the computer and the software for about $5000? I'd like to be ready to run by the beginning of the year.

Systems Analyst: Thanksgiving is next week! Why do I get into these things?

This is just a small part of the work necessary to properly define a complex program like a client data base. The actual program and hardware specifications might be developed in the course of several meetings spanning a month or more. If you work for a small programming or consulting firm, you may participate in all the stages of program development, from systems analysis to final testing.

Starting At the Top

There is a programming technique which is well-suited to translating system specifications into program code in Pascal. This is *top-down programming*. It simply means that you start by defining the most abstract goals of the program and work down to the most detailed code. The first steps in the generation of a client list program might look like this:

```
PROGRAM CLIENTLIST;
(* VARIABLE DECLARATIONS *)
(* AND PROCEDURES WILL GO *)
(* HERE AS THEY ARE WRITTEN *)
BEGIN
  REPEAT
    SHOWMENU;
    CASE SELECTION OF
      1: NEW CLIENTS;
      2: ENTERTRANSACTIONS;
      3: LISTCLIENTS;
      4: SHOWTRANSACTIONS;
      5: MAILINGLIST;
      6: BACKUPDISKS;
    END; (*OF CASE SELECTION*)
  UNTIL SELECTION = 7;
  SHUTDOWN;
END. (*CLIENTLIST MAIN PROGRAM*)
```

It is possible to start writing a BASIC program in the same way, but you would have to use REM statements to define the different modules. In Pascal, procedure names are used to indicate the job the code will accomplish.

Once you have defined the primary tasks of the program, in this case by giving them procedure names, you can go to the next level of detail. The procedure for the entry of new client data might look like this:

```
PROCEDURE NEWCLIENTS;
VAR    NCLIENT:CLIENTTYPE;
BEGIN
    SHOWFORM(CLIENTFORM);
    GETCLIENT(NCLIENT);
    ADDFILE(NCLIENT);
END;    (*NEWCLIENT*)
```

This procedure is a bit less abstract than the main menu definitions. A special type of data, CLIENTTYPE, is used as a parameter for two of the procedures. The procedures are called this way because it occurred to me that the same procedures might be used by other selections in the main menu. The process of defining the program elements would continue in this manner until the procedure could only be written as groups of the intrinsic procedures and functions of the Pascal language.

A Bit From the Bottom

At this time I'd like to point out an important deviation from the strict top-down programming sequence which will probably save you a lot of time and effort.

DEFINE DATA TYPES BEFORE PROGRAMMING

The major special types of data in a program should be defined before proceeding past the first step in the top-down sequence. In many cases it is best to define at least the names of the data types as part of the systems analysis.

The complex data types should be defined after the first run through the program in the top-down process because the type and amount of data plays a large part in determining the structure of the lowest level procedures in the program. This is particularly true when you write the procedures which ask for keyboard input or display the data on the screen. So a little bite from the bottom of the program—a preliminary, but careful, attempt to define the complex data types—will help fix the goals of the program more firmly in your mind.

When you have worked your way from the top to the bottom of the program for the first time, start looking for duplications and similarities among the different procedures. You will probably find several places where you can use the same procedure in several different parts of the program. If a procedure or function appears more than four or five times, consider adding it to a special library which can be separately compiled and called by the program.

Nesting

Pascal allows insertion of a complete procedure or function definition within the body of another procedure or function. When this is done, the inserted procedure is said to be *nested* within the outer procedure. The best reason for nesting procedures and functions is that the resulting code for the main part of the outer procedure will be simpler and easier to understand. Another reason for using procedure calls is to avoid writing the same block of code several times. A set of nested procedures might look like this:

```
PROCEDURE ADDREC(NEWTRANS:TRANSREC);
VAR TRANSFILE:FILE OF TRANSREC;
     FILERROR:BOOLEAN;

  PROCEDURE PUTTRANS(INSTOCK:TRANSREC;
                          RECNUM:INTEGER);
  BEGIN
    SEEK (TRANSFILE,RECNUM)
    TRANSFILE ∧: = NEWTRANS;
    PUT (TRANSFILE);
  END;    (*PUTTRANS*)

  PROCEDURE OPENTRANS;
```

```
BEGIN
  (*$I-*) (*DISABLE SYSTEM ERROR CHECKING*)
  RESET (TRANSFILE,'TRDISK:TRANSACTIONS.DATA');
  IF IORESULT< > 0 THEN FILERROR: = TRUE;
  (*$I + *)  (ENABLE SYSTEM ERROR CHECKING*)
END;   (*OPENTRANS*)


BEGIN   (*ADDREC MAIN PROCEDURE*)
  FILERROR: = FALSE;
  OPENTRANS;
  IF FILERROR THEN WRITELN('TRANSACTION FILE ERROR')
  ELSE
    BEGIN
      NEXTREC: = TRANSFILE∧.LINK;
      TRANSFILE∧.LINK: = TRANSFILE∧.LINK + 1;
      PUTTRANS(TRANSFILE∧,0);
      PUTTRANS(NEWTRANS,NEXTREC);
      CLOSE(TRANSFILE);
    END;
END;
```

In this example the OPENTRANS and PUTTRANS procedures are nested within the ADDREC procedure. Nested procedures cannot be called by any program element outside ADDREC. However, one of the nested procedures could call another which is at the same nesting level and which precedes the calling procedure in the source code. The nested procedures have access to all variables defined in the outer procedure or in the main program. A little later in this chapter we'll discuss *local* and *global* variables and clear up this business of which procedures can use which variables. When you decide to start nesting procedures, be careful that you don't keep some useful procedures from being used elsewhere in the program. This is certainly the case with the OPENTRANS procedure in the example. The transaction file will certainly be opened several other places in the main program. Therefore, this procedure should be a global procedure (at the same level as all the other menu selections in the main program). On the other hand, nesting the PUTTRANS procedure ensures that you will not accidentally write any code which puts spurious records into the data files. Nesting this procedure has, in effect, guaranteed that the ADDREC procedure is the only place where you can write to the data files.

Global Variables (They're Everywhere!)

Variables defined in the declarations section of the main program are called *global* variables. These variables may be used in the main program and any of its procedures—no matter how deeply they are nested. Any special data types defined in the main program declarations may also be used by all the procedures and functions in the program.

Global variables should be used with care. If a lot of global variables are defined, then used by many different procedures, there is a good chance that you will change the variable at one point, then use it in another procedure without remembering that the value was changed. This is called a *side-effect*. Over-use of global variables can lead to confusion and increased troubleshooting time. Many Pascal texts recommend that global variables be avoided completely and all variables be passed to procedures as explicit parameters. I agree with this principle, but disagree in two particular cases:

> 1. Variables which are read once and used many times in a program. An excellent example is the variable TODAY which would be a date entered once and used several times throughout the program. Another example is a large array of names read from a data file at the beginning of a program and used as a key for file accesses throughout the program.
>
> 2. Data files should be declared as global variables. It is essential that all program procedures agree on the structure and use of data files and it seems unnecessarily awkward to have to pass a file as a parameter. The alternative is to have each procedure define the file—which is a waste of time when all procedures should agree on the usage of the file in the first place.

When you do use global variables, change their values in only one or two modules of the program. If files are opened and written to only in a procedure called WRITEFILE, you aren't likely to call the procedure except when you want to change the file.

Any special data types which are used in more than one procedure should also be part of the global declarations. This will be necessary in the case of any data types used in files, since you have to define the types before the files are declared. Once you define these types, it is usually very handy to print a listing of the global declarations and pin it to the wall in a convenient spot where it can be used as a reference while you develop the rest of the program.

Local Variables

Variables which are defined within a procedure or function are called local variables. These variables have values defined only when the procedure is actually being executed. When procedures are nested, a variable defined in the outer procedure can be used by any procedures nested within it. In the ADDREC example, the variable FILERROR was a local variable defined only within that procedure. However, the FILERROR variable could also be used by the PUTTRANS procedure nested inside ADDREC.

When a local variable is defined which has the same name as a global variable, the local variable will be assigned a separate storage location from the global variable, and this location will be used for all references to the variable. Thus the local variable is said to "hide" the global variable. This may occur with such commonly used variable names as I,J,REC-NUM, etc., which are used as counters in many different locations.

The domain throughout which a particular variable may be referenced is known as the "scope" of the variable. A complete discussion of this subject is a little too complex and lengthy for this book.

The subject of local and global variables is a new one to most BASIC programmers, since that language treats all variables as global. The proper use of local variables can make your programs more readable and minimize programming effort.

Writing It Right the First Time

There are probably as many different ways of actually translating program ideas into executing code as there are programmers. Many programmers prefer to prepare elaborate flow charts (which may resemble maps of the Los Angeles freeway system) before writing a single line of code. Other programmers start with a blank pad of paper and, using a pen or pencil, write each line of code in the complete program before entering a single line at the terminal. Still others sit right down at the terminal and type the program in rather willy-nilly fashion—depending on the system editor to arrange the parts in the correct order later. I usually find myself in one of the latter two groups.

My personal approach to getting a program into the computer is to set the major details down on paper, then use the system's editor to compensate for my slow and often illegible handwriting. I can type at the terminal, even with backspacing to correct errors as they occur, at many times my handwriting rate. For this reason, I use handwritten notes, generally in the form of outlines or procedure skeletons, only when absolutely necessary.

There was probably a time (in the recent past) when programs were written on paper first because direct terminal access to the computer was limited and expensive. Thus, programs were written on paper, then punched on cards (keypunch time was also a limited commodity). The slow turn-around in these off-line programming situations placed a great premium on getting things right the first time. But, as we all know, few programs longer than 20 lines are completely correct the first time.

My emphasis on keyboard entry does not mean I have forsaken the paper record completely. Once I have entered a major part of any program, I then print a listing. This listing is used to check for logical and syntax errors and is generally covered with notes and corrections by the time the program first runs successfully. Long and complex programs may require several printouts and editing sessions.

As far as flow charts are concerned, I seldom use them. A well-designed Pascal program can be written in top-down fashion without them. About the only time I use flow charts is to think out a particularly complex nested test-and-loop sequence.

If you were born and raised in the academic world of flow charts and handwritten programs, you can regard the above paragraphs as the meanderings of an eccentric. By all means continue to write programs in the manner in which you get the best results. But don't get the idea that because colleges and universities use flow charts and punched cards, that is the only way to write good programs. In fact, I think you will find that many texts on Pascal are now devoting little attention to flow charts, preferring, instead, to give program examples whose structure and purpose is shown in the variable and procedure names.

11

Getting Along
with the System

When you use the UCSD Pascal system, you have to learn more than simply how to write Pascal programs. The Pascal compiler is only one part of a complete operating environment. In order to become an efficient programmer in this operating environment, you have to learn to use the editor, file manager and a number of other utility programs. This chapter will help you through some of the more difficult points in this transition to a new operating environment.

BASIC programming is generally carried out in a much more limited operating environment than is the case with the Pascal system. If you use a BASIC interpreter such as Applesoft, you carry out all your programming editing and file manipulations without ever leaving the BASIC interpreter. Applesoft and many other versions of BASIC allow you direct access to the operating system through commands recognized by the interpreter. The Apple and most other microcomputer systems have file management utilities and editors, but it is not really necessary to use them in preparing and running a BASIC program. In the Pascal system you cannot leave the editor and file manager until later—you have to be able to use them before you can write and run your first program. This chapter contains a brief description of some sticky details of the following elements of the Pascal operating system:

1. The file management utility

2. The text editor

3. The Pascal compiler

4. The program linking utility

5. System libraries and library managers

I will also discuss (though not in great detail), such topics as units, program chaining and specialized system libraries.

The Filer

The UCSD Pascal system provides a utility program called the Filer, which allows you to list the catalog of a diskette, change the names of files and transfer files from one diskette to another. Become familiar with this utility program before writing any programs. The manual which describes the use of the filer is both complete and accurate, but there are a few points about the use of this program that I would like to emphasize. The first of these is the matter of workfiles.

The Pascal system allows you to specify that a particular file name should be used as the default file for editing, compiling and running programs. This file is named SYSTEM . WRK . TEXT (or SYSTEM.WRK. CODE for a compiled code file). The filer allows you to use the GET command to specify a particular file as the workfile. The GET command does not actually transfer the contents of the named file to a file called SYSTEM .WRK, but only tells the system to use the named file *instead* of the SYSTEM . WRK file. If you use the text editor to change the workfile, then use the Update option to exit the editor program, you will actually create a file called SYSTEM . WRK . TEXT on your boot diskette. At this point the original file you named as the workfile remains unchanged on the diskette where it originally resided. You may update this file by transferring the contents of the SYSTEM . WRK file into it with the SAVE command in the filer.

This use of default workfiles has both advantages and disadvantages. The primary advantage to be found in the use of workfiles is that you won't have to specify file names each time you switch from editor to compiler and back as you develop a program. If you are developing a small

program which doesn't use included text files and can all be stored on your
boot diskette, workfiles can be a great timesaver.

Most of the advantages of workfiles are lost if you are developing a
program too large to fit into the system editor all at one time. If you break
up your source code into blocks joined together at compilation with an In-
clude-File statement (I'll cover that option when I discuss the Compiler),
you can only specify one part of the program as the workfile. A second
problem is that the system always wants to store the workfile on your boot
diskette. I find it much more convenient to put all my operating system
files and utilities on the boot diskette, and leave all the program text and
code files on separate disks. By the time I have put all the system files on an
Apple diskette, there are only about nine blocks (4.5 K bytes) left for the
workfile. This is not enough file space to be really useful to me.

For the reasons I've discussed above, I seldom use the Filer's Get and
Save commands to specify and manipulate workfiles. The concept of
workfiles seems well suited to the educational use of Pascal, where a student may develop one reasonably small program at a time. In a professional programming environment, I find it much more useful to clear the workfiles and name each file as I edit and compile it. Since I seldom use the
workfile capability, a most important Filer command is the Prefix command. This command allows you to prefix any file name with a default
volume name. This will usually be the name of the program disk in the second disk drive. For example, a prefix of UTIL: would cause the editor, filer,
and compiler always to look on my utilities disk for any files they would
need as input or output storage.

The filer may be the most often-used utility program in the Pascal system. Study the filer instructions carefully and learn to use this program
before writing any large or complex programs. The proper use of wild card
file designators and multiple-file transfers will help to make backup copies
of important files quickly and efficiently. The filer is also used to transfer
text files to the system line printer. The printer is treated as a file used for
output only. You can also treat such devices as modems as remote input
and output files. The details of the utilization of such devices are beyond
the scope of this book. I'll end this discussion of the Filer with a warning
note. It is often tempting to make a backup copy of an important data disk
with a full-volume copy statement like:

#4:,#5:

which should transfer the complete contents (directory included) of the
diskette in drive #1 (volume #4) to drive #2. (When you refer to a device by

number or a diskette volume by name and use only the name or number followed by a colon, you refer to the complete contents of the volume. If you are puzzled by volume names and numbers, please consult your operating system manuals before proceeding further.) If the diskette in drive #2 is a newly initialized disk (with volume name BLANK:), this procedure works very well. But you can get into trouble the next time you try this backup procedure when the system finds that it has two diskettes in different drives which have the same volume name. The Pascal system manuals warn you about this situation, and rightly so. You may get away with this transfer four times out of five, but the fifth time you will probably get a message like "Volume went off line." If it happens to be one of those days when nothing works right, you may mess up the directory of either or both of the diskettes. For this reason I recommend the following procedure when making full-disk backups:

1. Write-protect the original disk.

2. Change the name of the backup volume to Blank: or something equally innocuous. (Be sure the original is not in either drive.)

3. Put the original in drive #1 and the backup in drive #2, then transfer the complete diskette.

I could probably continue for another four or five pages describing exactly how I use the filer in my programming, but I'm pretty sure you will have your own preferences for volume names, file names, and when and how to make backups (often!). The filer is a vital utility program and you should become familiar with it very quickly. The manuals describing its use (at least in the UCSD system) are clear and concise. A little reading and some practice will help immensely as you manipulate larger program and data files.

The Editor

The text editor provided with the UCSD Pascal system is probably one of the best on the market if you are looking for an editor designed to prepare program source code. This editor has many features, such as automatic indentation, the ability to insert text from disk files, and a full range of text manipulation commands, which combine to make it a powerful and versatile tool for the preparation of programs. While it is not designated primarily as a word-processing editor, it can, by changing certain parameters, be used to prepare text for letters, forms and manuals. The Apple Pascal operating system manual devotes more than 50 pages to instruction on the use of the editor. I won't attempt to describe it in that much detail. There are two aspects of the use of the editor which will require a little practice before you become completely comfortable with its operation. The first of these is the Set Environment command. This command allows you to modify parameters which affect the manner in which the editor will format and display the text you enter. When entering program source code, you will probably want neatly indented lines of text. I like to indent each new level of nesting in a program by two spaces. I find that two-space indentation is visually distinctive enough to show the level of nesting without making the lines so long that many of them are more than 80 characters wide. The Auto-Indent option in the environment setting mode allows you to format your source code neatly. When you type a carriage return at the end of a program line, the next line begins at the same position as the last entered line. If you wish to step to the left to remove a level of nesting, use the backspace key immediately after the carriage return. If the AUTO-INDENT mode were set to FALSE, you would have to indent each line manually as it was typed—a terrific waste of time. Auto-indentation would normally be turned off for preparation of letters and forms where each line might have a different indentation. Another set of commands allows you to set the margins to be used by the editor. The editor normally warns you when you approach the right margin by beeping the computer's speaker when you are within nine characters of the end of the line. If you use a standard Apple to enter text, you can use various commands to display either the left or right half of the 80-column display, or display the part of the screen which contains the cursor. If you have a system with an 80-column display, you can see the complete line of text as it is entered.

The SET ENVIRONMENT command also allows selection of a line-filling mode. This mode is normally set to FALSE when entering program source lines. If the FILL mode is activated, you can enter several lines of text without intervening carriage returns. When this mode is active the editor will automatically enter carriage returns whenever the word you enter exceeds the specified right margin. This command, along with the capability to reformat the margins of a paragraph of text automatically, make the editor much more useful for entering and editing letters, manuals and other text which doesn't require the special indentation and formatting which make programs easier to read and understand.

The Compiler

The compiler is the program which is the heart of the Pascal system. This program reads a source code file and converts the program into pseudo-code which will be executed when the program is run. The compiler checks the syntax of the program, allocates storage for programs and variables and writes the resulting pseudo-code into a code file on a diskette. If you are not using a workfile, the compiler will ask you to provide the names of the input text file and the name to be used for the output code file. There are a number of other optional controls you can use to modify the operation of the compiler, and I'd like to discuss a few of the most important of these.

Compiler options are embedded in the source code of the program as a special form of a comment. The "$" character immediately following the left-hand comment delimiter indicates to the compiler than an option command follows. Here are the compiler options I have found most useful:

> (*$I − *) and (*$I + *). These two options tell the compiler whether or not to include code which will check the validity of any input or output operations. When I/O checking is on (I +, the normal default mode), the compiler will generate code to verify each I/O operation and halt with a run-time error message if there is any problem with the I/O. If I/O checking is turned off with the I- option, it becomes your responsibility to check each I/O operation and take appropriate action if there is an error. I use this option to ensure that the proper diskettes are in the drives before reading or writing information in disk files. A good example of the use of this option can be found in the OPENTRANS procedure in the previous chapter.
>
> **The Include-File Mechanism.** The Pascal compiler can be instructed to include another source file into the compilation with a command such as:
>
> (*$ITRANSTUFF.TEXT*)
>
> When the compiler reaches this option in the original source file, it would open the TRANSTUFF file, then read and compile all the text before reading any further input from the original file. This option makes it possible to compile programs when the source code is too long to fit in the editor (the editor will only work with about 17,000 bytes of text at a time).
>
> **Listing Options.** You may direct the compiler to prepare an annotated source listing while it compiles a program. This listing contains information such as the line, segment and procedure numbers corresponding to each line of the source code. This listing can be very useful in tracing run-time errors. The two most common versions of this option are:
>
> (*$LCONSOLE:*)
>   and
> (*$LPRINTER:*)

The first sends the listing to the video terminal, and the second prints the listing on the line printer. This command may appear anywhere in the body of the source text. The listing can be discontinued at any time with the (*$L − *) option.

Swapping Mode.   The Pascal compiler is a very large program. When the whole compiler is loaded into memory, it has only a few thousand words of space free for maintaining a table of the symbols and addresses generated by the program being compiled. The swapping option causes the compiler to read certain parts of itself from the boot diskette each time they are needed. In this way, several different parts of the compiler are able to use the same memory space at different times. As a result, there is more space left for symbols from the program being compiled. The disadvantage of using this option is that compilation is slowed down because the compiler must read parts of itself from the disk while it runs. You will probably find that swapping is necessary for any program which has more than about 200 lines of source code. The swapping options are as follows:

(*S + *)   Start swapping mode—should be used at the start of the program.

(*S + + *)   Engage another level of swapping which frees even more memory for the user. (I haven't had to resort to this option—even in programs longer than 1000 lines.)

(*S − *)   Set non-swapping mode. This is the default setting. I never turn swapping off once it is on.

These and some other less often used compiler options allow a great deal of control over the compilation of programs. One of the nicer features of the compiler is that it reports any syntax errors in the program with a full description of the error. To do this, it reads a description of the error from a file named SYSTEM .SYNTAX on the boot diskette. If you do not have this file on the diskette (I don't, since I needed the room for another program), you get only an error number from the compiler. After about a year of programming, you learn certain error numbers by heart—like Syntax Error #6—which means I left out the semicolon at the end of a statement.

The Linker

The linker is a utility program which allows you to connect separately-compiled programs into a single block of code which the computer can execute. This program allows you to start with a compiled Pascal program which references external procedures or functions, then add the required routines from either the system library or a special library of routines of your own. The linker can be used to connect programs written in assembly language to your Pascal program. It can also be used to link pre-compiled Pascal program blocks, called *units,* into your main program. Writing assembly-language programs compatible with Pascal is an art I have yet to master, so I'll leave that subject for a later book. For now, I'll concentrate on units and user libraries.

A user library is a file which contains blocks of compiled Pascal code called units. A unit is a group of Pascal procedures and functions written in a slightly different form from a normal program. A unit consists of two major parts: an *interface* section and an *implementation* section.

The interface section of a unit consists of a standard declarations section — the constants, type and variable definitions in this section may be used by the program which calls the unit just as if they were part of the main program. The interface also contains a list of the names of all the procedures and functions in the unit, complete with the parameters they use to communicate with the program.

The implementation section of the unit consists of constant, type and variable declarations which are local to the unit—they cannot be used by the main program. This section also contains the actual code for each of the procedures and functions in the unit. A very simple unit might look like this:

```
UNIT PRINTSTUFF;

INTERFACE
    CONST        PNAME = 'PRINTER:';
    VAR          OUTDEV:TEXT;

    PROCEDURE    OPENPRINT;
    PROCEDURE    PRINTLINE(PSTRING:STRING);

IMPLEMENTATION

    PROCEDURE  OPENPRINT;
    BEGIN
        REWRITE(OUTDEV,PNAME);
    END;    (*OPENPRINT*)
```

```
    PROCEDURE PRINTLINE; (*NO PARAMETERS HERE*)
    BEGIN
       WRITELN(OUTDEV,PSTRING);
    END;    (*PRINTLINE*)


  BEGIN
    (*THIS DUMMY BEGIN-END PAIR IS REQUIRED TO *)
    (*KEEP THINGS STRAIGHT DURING COMPILATION AND*)
    (*LINKING*)
  END.
```

This unit could either be installed in the system library or into a separate user library. The unit is referenced at the beginning of the main program with a statement like:

```
    USES PRINTSTUFF;
```

If the unit is in a user library, you must tell the compiler the name of the library before it gets to the USES statement. The library name is defined with a compiler option, the user library option, which looks like this:

```
    (*U$  MYLIBRARY.CODE*)
```

There are three different types of units defined in the UCSD Pascal system. They are:

Intrinsic Units.   These units must always be installed in the system library. They are "pre-linked" and you will not have to use the linker with them. But you will have to make sure the system library is available when you run programs with intrinsic units. There are a number of special restrictions on how these units may be written. Check your system manuals for the details.

Regular Units.   Regular units are connected into the code file of the main program with the linker when you first run the program. These units may come from either the system library or a user library. Code from the unit is actually written into the code file for the main program when the unit is linked. Thus the library unit does not have to be available after the first time you link and run the program.

Separate Units.   A separate unit is like a regular unit, except that only the functions and procedures actually used in the main program are linked into the code file. Thus if you only used two or three procedures from a large library, you would not have to include the code from the unused routines in the code file. This could save a lot of space in the code file and in memory when the program was run. Unfortunately, this type of unit is not supported in the Apple version of UCSD Pascal. It may be supported on other computers.

When you use the linker to add routines from a library to your code file, the program will ask for the name of the host file—your main program code file. It will then ask for the name of the library file where it can find the referenced units. You can specify more than one library if you have several USES statements referencing different libraries. After you have named all the libraries, the program asks whether you want a map file. A map file can be written which will contain information about the linking process. If you want to see this map, it is usually easiest to specify PRINTER: as the file name (remember that the line printer looks like a file to the operating system). The linker will also ask for the name of the file which receives the output code.

This description of the linker and the units and libraries it works with should give you a running start if you decide to use separate libraries in your programs. These libraries can save a lot of time when you are working on a long program. By putting all the low level procedures in the library (the procedures you define last in the top-down approach), you can save a lot of compiling time while you work on the main program. Any modification of the main program will consist mostly of changes in the order in which the procedures in the library are used.

Miscellaneous Utilities

The UCSD system provides a number of utility programs to help you manage files and programs. The most important of these are:

The Formatter.   This program allows you to initialize new diskettes on systems like the Apple, which must write their own special track and sector formats on new diskettes. Systems which use standard 8-inch, IBM-format diskettes may not need this program at all.

The Librarian.   This program is used to build a new library file. It allows you to make up a new library with units drawn from the system library and other units you have written and compiled.

The Library Mapper.   This utility program writes a map of a library file to the file designated (usually the printer). The program will write all the information in the interface portion of a library file. This allows you to refresh your memory when you aren't sure just which routines are included in the current version of a library.

There may be several other utility routines delivered with your version of the Pascal system. The programs included may be very specifically oriented to your particular computer. Since I have access to only a limited number of the different computers on the market, I'll have to leave a little of the exploring to you.

I hope this chapter has given you a better understanding of the different programs that make up the complete UCSD Pascal operating system. If you write any long and complex programs, you have to get to know your Pascal utilities as well as you know your BASIC interpreter. After your programs reach a length of about 500 lines, you will find that included files and separately compiled and linked units will be great timesavers — and that's what good programming is all about—saving you time and the time of everyone who uses your programs.

12

. . . And a Few Words in Closing

This chapter covers about a half-dozen subjects with a light coat of white-wash. I'll discuss some features of Pascal that you probably won't use in your first programs, but should know about for future reference. When it comes time to use these features, consult your Pascal reference manuals and a book or two that cover advanced programming in more detail.

Graphics, Music and Other Geegaws

Graphics routines are built into the UCSD Pascal system and are im-plemented on the Apple II and some other computers which have graphics capability. The graphics routines are contained in a portion of the system library called TURTLESTUFF. When you link this code into your program you can use procedures like MOVETO, TURNTO, PENCOLOR and FILLSCREEN to draw pictures on the video screen.

The graphics routines can be used to draw charts, graphs or even pic-tures on the console screen. Where Applesoft BASIC had no capability to put text characters on the screen, Pascal allows you to write characters and strings anywhere on the graphics display. The graphics capabilities of Pascal are generally much improved over those in BASIC, but are still limited by the same restrictions:

> 1. The resolution of the video screen (on the Apple or any other system which uses a standard television for display) is not great enough for most scientific or engineering applications. The television is limited to about 280 points across the screen and 192 vertical lines. Even an inexpensive flat-bed plotter has a resolution of 1600 to 2000 points across an 8½ by 11-inch sheet of paper.

> 2. There are no built-in capabilities to produce hard-copy pictures from the screen image. This is a problem that should soon be solved. Many manufacturers of dot-matrix printers with graphics capability are now offering routines to convert screen images to black-and-white pictures by calling a machine-language routine in BASIC. I suspect that these routines will soon be available for Pascal.

Just as there are people who feel graphics displays are important, there are others who place a high premium on a computer's ability to make unusual noises. The Apple and other systems with built-in speakers may allow you to program the system to generate tones of a specific pitch and duration. This is far from a general-purpose music generation capability. Systems which use built-in speakers all suffer from the fact that these speakers are two inches in diameter, hidden inside the computer, and often cause parts of the computer to resonate in a very annoying manner. If you must use your computer to make music, invest in one of the several excellent music peripherals available. As far as producing music, a friend insists that a piano not only sounds better, but the keyboard is more logically arranged. I can't help but agree with her. You may find that the pitch-generation capability is useful for generating distinctive audible warnings, but a series of one or more bell characters is usually enough to catch the operator's attention.

The Apple and many other personal computers are extensively used for game playing. Very few games are written in Pascal at this time, but the system does have the capability of reading data from the game paddles and their associated buttons. These paddles find little, if any, use in business, scientific or engineering programs. Perhaps their greatest utility is as an input device for graphics programs. To read the game paddles on the Apple you must include a unit called APPLESTUFF in your program. This unit allows you to use functions and procedures to generate random numbers, read the game paddles, activate the Apple's TTL logic outputs and generate the tones discussed in the previous paragraph. (If the word "unit" confuses you, persevere until I discuss program libraries.) The APPLESTUFF unit does contain one very useful function, KEYPRESS, which returns a Boolean result of TRUE if a keyboard key has been pressed. This function is used to test for operator interruptions of looping routines—in order to terminate a long display sequence, for instance. Since I often do not want to include the whole APPLESTUFF unit into my program just to get the KEYPRESS function, I usually include my own short function which has the same result:

```
FUNCTION KEYPRESS:BOOLEAN;
TYPE BYTES = PACKED ARRAY[0..1]OF 0..255;
VAR TRIX:RECORD
  CASE BOOLEAN OF
    FALSE:(ADDRESS:INTEGER);
    TRUE :(POINTER:∧BYTES);
  END;

BEGIN
  TRIX.ADDRESS: = - 16384; (*KEYBOARD FLAG*)
  KEYPRESS: = TRIX.POINTER∧[0]>127;
  (*FUNCTION IS TRUE IF BYTE >127*)
END;
```

This function works only on the Apple, since it directly accesses a memory location which is the keyboard data register. The function also uses two new programming devices, the variant record and the pointer variable, which are seldom used (at least in my programs), but do deserve a little explanation.

Variant Records

The variant record is simply an extension of the record variable which was discussed in chapter 5. A record of this type consists of one or more fixed fields, just like a standard record, and a single variant field. The variant field may take on the characteristics of one of a number of variable types. The different variable types which the variant field may become are generally selected with a CASE statement. A program to catalog astronomical bodies might have a record like this:

```
TYPE ASTROBODY:RECORD
    CATNUMBER:INTEGER;
    BODYTYPE:(STAR,PLANET,MOON,ASTEROID);
    DIAMETER:REAL;
    CASE BODYTYPE OF
        STAR:(STARTYPE:INTEGER);
        PLANET:(ALBEDO:REAL);
        MOON:(ALBEDO:REAL);
        ASTEROID:(ALBEDO:REAL);
    END;    (*OF CASE STATEMENT*)
END; (*OF RECORD*)
```

This record uses the BODYTYPE variable to select whether the record should have associated with it a star type (which would indicate the brightness and color of the star's light or an albedo (a measure of the body's ability to reflect light). The BODYTYPE part of the record is called the *tag field*. The value of the tag field is used in the CASE statement to determine which variable type will be used in the variant part of the record.

Only one variant field may be used in the list of field types for a record. You can, however, include in a field list a field type which is itself a record with its own variant field. Nesting of variant records in this manner should be carefully considered (and usually rejected), as you may end up with records which are so complex that the clarity and precision of your program may be severely damaged.

The variant field in a record must always be the last field in the record and the record will always occupy enough space so that the longest variant field can be accommodated. Thus, if two of the variants are integers (2 bytes) and one is a 20-character string (21 bytes), the variant part of the record will always occupy 21 bytes. This can lead to a lot of wasted memory and file space if the longer type of variant is seldom used.

Dynamic Variables and Pointers

Throughout this book we have assumed that all variables are defined in a declarations section before the program is run. These variables are called *static* variables and the declarations allow the computer to allocate a fixed amount of space on the system stack before the program or procedure is executed. A second class of variables, the *dynamic* variable, can also be used in Pascal. The storage for a dynamic variable is not allocated until the program reaches the statement where it is defined. The statement used to define a dynamic variable is:

    NEW(VARTYPE);

where the parameter is a type definition, generally for an array or a record.

One of the components of the array or record must be a special type called a *pointer*. This type of variable is very useful in defining data structures known as *lists*—another subject beyond the scope of this book. The dynamic variable is created in an area of memory called the *heap* in UCSD Pascal. This is an area of memory where temporary and dynamic variables are stored and usually starts at the low end of memory and grows upward. Static variables, including local variable and parameters passed to procedures, are placed on the *stack*—an area of memory which expands downward from the top of the free memory as procedures are called and terminated. (When Pascal gives you a *stack overflow error*, it means that the stack has expanded downward into the heap or into special areas of memory reserved for machine-language operation—the 6502 microprocessor's hardware stack, for instance.)

The details of the implementation and use of dynamic variables and pointers are beyond the scope of this book. The central element in the KEYPRESS example is that a pointer variable (designated with the ↑ or up-arrow) can be used to point to a specific memory location. Pascal programs are generally well-insulated from the specifics of actual memory locations—a feature which makes them easier to move between computers with different memory organizations. Pointer variables can be used to trick (thus the TRIX variable name) the operating system into returning the value of a specific memory location.

The KEYPRESS function is the only case where I have had to use a pointer variable—and even then I could have used a machine-language or library routine. The Pascal routine was easier because it did not require a separate assembly step or a mostly-useless library module. If you write business or scientific data management programs, use dynamic variables and pointers with extreme caution. There are several reasons for this advice:

1. It can be hard to keep track of dynamic variables. If you lose track of them they clutter up the computer's memory.

2. Data structures built with a dynamic variable are limited in size by the amount of free memory available. You will generally be better off with a

disk file which simulates a dynamic structure, but can be several times larger.

3. Dynamic data structures disappear when your program crashes—from an accidental RESET, a power glitch, or (Heaven forbid!) a programming error. A data structure on diskette will generally remain intact if you are careful about closing the file after each use.

Libraries

Pascal allows the programmer to compile often-used procedures and functions and place them in special files called libraries. These procedures are then linked into a program before it is run. If you are working on a long program, the time required to edit, compile, and test the program can be significantly reduced if portions of the program are placed into a library as they are completed and tested.

The UCSD Operating system allows the use of two different types of libraries. The first of these is the *system library*, used by the Pascal system itself. It contains portions of code, called *units*, used to carry out disk reading and writing, generation of transcendental functions (sine, cosine, etc.), and manipulation of long integers. The library may also have units for graphics and special system-dependent functions such as the APPLE-STUFF unit for the Apple.

The second type of library is the *user library*, a file set up by the programmer which contains units of code which you can use in your own programs. The Pascal program is told to search for routines in a user library with a special form of comment called a compiler option. To instruct the system to search a library called MYLIBRARY, use a command like this:

```
(*$U MYLIBRARY*)
```

Once you have defined a new library (or left the library as SYSTEM . LIBRARY by default), tell the operating system which units you wish to use from the library. This is done with the USES command:

```
USES IOPACK,SCREENFORMAT;
```

which allows the program to use routines that provide special disk input and output and screen formatting procedures.

It is also possible to add new units or delete unused units from existing libraries. Your Pascal system should come with utility programs called LIBRARY . CODE and LIBMAP . CODE. The first of these allows you to change the contents of libraries and the second allows you to get a listing of the titles and characteristics of the procedures and functions in each unit of a library.

The way in which units are written and the different types of units are, once again, beyond the scope of this book. There are some differences in the manner in which units are implemented on various computers, so be sure to study your system manuals thoroughly before proceeding with libraries and units.

The Last Word

Well, you've done it! You've made it to the last pages of this book. Unless you're the type who skips to the end of a murder mystery before reading the clues, you've learned about the similarities and differences between BASIC and Pascal. I've tried to impress you with some of the strengths of Pascal and show you how to apply what you've learned in programming in BASIC to this new language. Since I've concentrated on the type of programming that will be used in business and scientific data management, I have omitted many of the details of Pascal that make it such a versatile language. On the other hand, a book which covers all these details soon becomes more like an encyclopedia than an introductory manual. When you have finished this book, visit a library or computer store and look through the Pascal books on the shelves. I am sure you will find several which will answer some of the questions I have raised in this brief attempt to help you make the transition from BASIC to Pascal.

Appendix I

Some Useful
Procedures

This appendix contains a number of procedures and functions which you may find useful in your own programs. Most of these are concerned with input and output, since these are the areas which have the most in common among different types of programs. I cannot hope to anticipate the exact data manipulations you will be using in your programs, but I can be reasonably certain that you will have to use some of the fundamental data types these program segments allow you to manipulate. This appendix contains a description of each procedure or function and the source code for it. These procedures may all be put into a pre-compiled system library where you may call them whenever you need them in your applications programs. Be sure to check your system manual for the difference in format between in-line procedures (as these are written) and procedure in separately compiled units.

Data Types

The following special data types are used in many of the procedures and functions in this appendix. When you add these routines to your programs, you must also add these declarations:

```
TYPE
    SETOFCHAR = SET OF CHAR;

    MONTH = 1 . . 12;
    DAY = 1 . . 31;
    YEAR = 0 . . 99;

    BUCKTYPE:INTEGER[8];
```

Keypress Function

The following KEYPRESS function is specially designed for the AP-PLE II computer. It actually checks a special hardware location which is the keyboard input register. It is one of the few times I have had occasion to use a pointer variable. The function is useful only for testing to see whether a single key has been pressed, since it will not add characters to the type-ahead buffer normally maintained by Pascal.

```
FUNCTION KEYPRESS:BOOLEAN;
TYPE BYTES = PACKED ARRAY[0 . . 1]OF 0 . . 255;
VAR TRIX:RECORD
    CASE BOOLEAN OF
        FALSE :(ADDRESS:INTEGER);
        TRUE  :(POINTER:^BYTES);
    END;

BEGIN
    TRIX . ADDRESS: = − 16384;
    KEYPRESS: = TRIX . POINTER ^[0] >127;
END;
```

Delay Procedure

The DELAY procedure is used whenever you want to pause during output to allow someone to read the screen. The procedure will pause about one second for each 500 units of delay time.

```
PROCEDURE DELAY(DTIME:INTEGER);


VAR I:INTEGER;
BEGIN
   FOR I: = 1 TO DTIME DO;
END;
```

String Entry from the Console

The GETCHAR function is used to get a single character from the keyboard. The keyboard input character must be an element of the set of characters specified in the input character set OKSET. If the character is not valid, the bell character is transmitted (a beep on the Apple speaker). If the character is valid, it is displayed on the screen and returned as the function value. This routine is used by many of the following keyboard input procedures. Please note that the global variable type SETOFCHAR: SET OF CHAR; must be defined at the beginning of the program.

```
FUNCTION     GETCHAR(OKSET:SETOFCHAR);
VAR CH: CHAR;
   GOOD: BOOLEAN;
BEGIN
   REPEAT
      READ(KEYBOARD,CH);
      IF EOLN(KEYBOARD) THEN CH: = CHR(13);
      GOOD: = CH IN OKSET;
      IF NOT GOOD THEN WRITE(CHR(7))
         ELSE IF CH IN ['  '..'}'] THEN WRITE(CH);
   UNTIL GOOD;
   GETCHAR: = CH;
END;
```

The YES function is the simplest use of the GETCHAR function. This function returns a Boolean result of TRUE if an upper or lower-case 'Y' is entered from the keyboard. An entry of 'N' or 'n' returns a FALSE value. No other keyboard entries are accepted.

```
FUNCTION YES:BOOLEAN;
BEGIN
   YES: = GETCHAR(['Y','y','N','n'])   IN ['Y','y'];
END;
```

GETSTRING is a special input routine which allows the user to enter a string from the keyboard. The routine may be called with a default input string passed into the procedure. If the user simply types a carriage return, the default string is accepted as the new string. If any other character is entered, the new string will be returned. When a default string is passed to the procedure, then a new string started, the procedure displays a row of periods showing the maximum length of the input string. The length of the string is also a parameter passed to the procedure.

```
PROCEDURE GETSTRING(VAR S:STRING;    MAXLEN:INTEGER);
VAR S1:   STRING[1];
    I:INTEGER;
    STEMP:   STRING[80];
    OKSET:   SET OF CHAR;
BEGIN
 OKSET: = ['   '..'}'];
 S1: = '   ';
 STEMP: = '';
 REPEAT
 IF LENGTH(STEMP) = 0 THEN S1[1]: = GETCHAR(OKSET + [CHR(13)])
    ELSE IF LENGTH(STEMP) = MAXLEN THEN S1[1]: = GETCHAR ([CHR(13), CHR(8)])
       ELSE S1[1]: = GETCHAR(OKSET + [CHR(13), CHR(8)]);
 IF S1[1] IN OKSET THEN STEMP: = CONCAT(STEMP,S1)
    ELSE IF S1[1] = CHR(8) THEN
      BEGIN
        WRITE(S1[1]);
        DELETE(STEMP,LENGTH(STEMP),1);
      END;
```

```
IF LENGTH(STEMP) = 1 THEN
   BEGIN
      FOR I: = 1 TO MAXLEN – 1 DO WRITE('.');
      FOR I: = 1 TO MAXLEN – 1 DO WRITE(CHR(8));
   END;
UNTIL S1[1] = CHR(13);
IF LENGTH(STEMP)< >0 THEN S: = STEMP
ELSE WRITE(S);
END;
```

Entry of a Date from the Console

The DATSTRING procedure is a slight modification of the GET-STRING procedure used to input a string to be converted to a date. The only input characters allowed are the digits 0-9 and the '/' character as a separator. The maximum length of the string is fixed at eight characters.

```
PROCEDURE DATSTRING(VAR NSTRING:STRING);
VAR S1: STRING[1];
    STEMP: STRING[8];
    OKSET: SET OF CHAR;
    I:INTEGER;
    DIGITS:SET OF CHAR;
BEGIN
 DIGITS: = ['0'..'9'];
 OKSET: = DIGITS + ['/'];
 S1: = ' ';
 STEMP: = '';
 REPEAT
    IF LENGTH(STEMP) = 0 THEN S1[1]: = GETCHAR (OKSET + [CHR(13)])
       ELSE IF LENGTH(STEMP) = 8 THEN S1[1]: = GETCHAR([CHR(13),CHR(8)])
          ELSE S1[1]: = GETCHAR(OKSET + [CHR(13),CHR(8)]);
    IF S1[1] IN OKSET THEN STEMP: = CONCAT(STEMP,S1)
       ELSE IF S1[1] = CHR(8) THEN
          BEGIN
             WRITE(S1[1]);
             DELETE(STEMP,LENGTH(STEMP),1);
          END;
```

```
      IF LENGTH(STEMP) = 1 THEN
         BEGIN
            FOR I: = 1 TO 7 DO WRITE ('.');
            FOR I: = 1 TO 7 DO WRITE(CHR(8));
         END;
   UNTIL S1[1] = CHR(13);
   NSTRING: = STEMP
END;
```

The next procedure actually accepts a date from the keyboard. It calls the DATSTRING procedure to accept the entry. Before the string is entered the cursor is positioned on the screen by the XLIN and YLIN parameters. If an error is made in entering the date, a message is printed on line 22 of the screen, and the date must be re-entered. The procedure does not check for erroneous dates as 2/31/81 since it will allow any month to have as many as 31 days.

```
PROCEDURE  GETDATE(VAR ADATE:DATREC;   XLIN,YLIN:INTEGER);
VAR DPOS,M,D,Y:INTEGER;
    DELIM:STRING[1];
    DTSTRING:DSTRING;
    ERROR:BOOLEAN;
BEGIN
 DSTRING: = '';
 REPEAT
   DELIM: = '/';
   ERROR: =FALSE;
   GOTOXY(XLIN,YLIN);
   DATSTRING(DTSTRING);
   IF LENGTH(DTSTRING)< >0 THEN
      BEGIN
         DPOS: = POS(DELIM,DTSTRING);
         IF (DPOS< >2)AND(DPOS< > 3) THEN ERROR: = TRUE
         ELSE
            BEGIN
               IF DPOS = 2 THEN M: = ORD(DTSTRING[1]) – ORD('0')
               ELSE M: = 10*(ORD(DTSTRING[1]) – ORD('0'))
                  + ORD(DTSTRING[2]) – ORD('0');
               DELETE(DTSTRING,1,DPOS);
```

```
            END;
        DPOS: = POS (DELIM,DTSTRING);
        IF (DPOS<>2)AND(DPOS<>3) THEN ERROR: = TRUE
        ELSE
            BEGIN
                IF DPOS = 2 THEN D: = ORD(DTSTRING[1]) – ORD('0')
                ELSE D: = 10*(ORD (DTSTRING[1]) – ORD ('0'))
                    + ORD(DTSTRING[2]) – ORD('0');
                DELETE(DTSTRING,1,DPOS);
            END;
        IF LENGTH (DTSTRING)<>2 THEN ERROR: = TRUE
        ELSE Y: = 10*(ORD(DTSTRING[1]) – ORD('0'))
            + ORD (DTSTRING[2]) – ORD('0');
        IF (M<1) OR (M>12) THEN ERROR: = TRUE;
        IF (Y<0) OR (Y>99) THEN ERROR: = TRUE;
        IF (D<1) OR (D>31) THEN ERROR: = TRUE;
        IF ERROR = TRUE THEN
            BEGIN
                GOTOXY(0,22);
                WRITELN(CHR(7),'DATE INPUT ERROR');
                GOTOXY(XLIN,YLIN);
            END;
    END;   (*IF LENGTH<>0*)
 UNTIL ERROR = FALSE;
 IF LENGTH(DTSTRING)<>0 THEN
    BEGIN
        ADATE.MM: = M;
        ADATE.YY: = Y;
        ADATE.DD: = D;
    END;
END;   (*GETDATE*)
```

Printing a Number as Dollars and Cents

The WRITEBUCKS procedure prints out a long integer as a formatted number in dollars and cents. The number is always displayed with two digits after the decimal point and is right-justified in a field 12 spaces wide.

```
PROCEDURE WRITEBUCKS(BUCKS:BUCKTYPE);
VAR ASTRING:STRING[30];
      SLEN:INTEGER;
BEGIN
   STR(BUCKS,ASTRING);
   INSERT('.',ASTRING,LENGTH(ASTRING) - 1);
   ASTRING' = CONCAT('              ',ASTRING);
   SLEN: = LENGTH(ASTRING);
   ASTRING: = COPY(ASTRING,SLEN - 11,12);
   WRITE(ASTRING);
END;   (*WRITEBUCKS*)
```

Entering Numbers at the Console

The next group of procedures allows the user to enter numbers from the keyboard without risking a program crash if the number is improperly entered. The procedures check for such errors as alphabetic characters in the input, multiple points, etc. Note that the procedures only allow the entry of positive numbers. Business programs for which they were written have other methods for deciding whether the number will be added to, or subtracted from, a total. The first procedure, NUMSTRING, allows the entry of the number string. Like the GETSTRING procedure, it accepts a default input string which will be accepted if only a carriage return is entered.

```
PROCEDURE   NUMSTRING(VAR NSTRING:STRING);
VAR S1:   STRING[1];
    STEMP:   STRING[11];
    I:INTEGER;
    OKSET: SET OF CHAR;
    DIGITS:SET OF CHAR;
```

```
BEGIN
  DIGITS: = ['0'..'9'];
  OKSET: = DIGITS + ['.'];
  S1: = '  ':
  STEMP: = '';
  REPEAT
      IF LENGTH(STEMP) = 0 THEN S1[1]: = GETCHAR(OKSET + [CHR(13)])
          ELSE IF LENGTH(STEMP) = 10 THEN S1[1]: = GETCHAR([CHR(13),CHR(8)])
              ELSE S1[1]: = GETCHAR(OKSET + [CHR(13),CHR(8)]);
      IF S1[1] IN OKSET THEN STEMP: = CONCAT(STEMP,S1)
          ELSE IF S1[1] = CHR(8) THEN
              BEGIN
                  WRITE(S1[1]);
                  IF STEMP [LENGTH(STEMP)] = '.' THEN OKSET: = DIGITS + ['.'];
                  DELETE(STEMP,LENGTH(STEMP),1);
              END;
      IF S1[1] = '.' THEN OKSET: = DIGITS;
      IF LENGTH(STEMP) = 1 THEN
          BEGIN
              FOR I: = 1 TO 7 DO WRITE('.');
              FOR I: = 1 TO 7 DO WRITE(CHR(8));
          END;
      UNTIL S1[1] = CHR(13);
      NSTRING: = STEMP;
  END;
```

The GETREAL procedure returns a positive real number from the keyboard. The procedure builds a very large integer number first, then scales it down by dividing the integer by ten for each digit entered after the decimal point.

```
PROCEDURE GETREAL(VAR RNUM:REAL);
VAR SPOS,SCALE,SFACT,COUNT:INTEGER;
    RSTRING:STOCKNAME;
    PNUM:REAL;
```

```
BEGIN
 NUMSTRING(RSTRING);
 IF LENGTH(RSTRING) < > 0 THEN
   BEGIN
      SCALE: = 0;
      SFACT: = 0;
      PNUM: = 0;
      FOR SPOS: = 1 TO LENGTH(RSTRING) DO
        BEGIN
          IF RSTRING[SPOS] = '.' THEN SFACT: = 1
          ELSE
            BEGIN
              PNUM: = PNUM*10 + ORD(RSTRING[SPOS]) – ORD('0');
              SCALE: = SCALE + SFACT;
            END;
          END;   (*FOR SPOS*)
        FOR COUNT: = 1 TO SCALE DO
          PNUM: = PNUM/10;
        RNUM: = PNUM;
      END;
 END;
```

The GETBUCK procedure allows the entry of a dollar amount from the keyboard. The result is a long integer with a maximum of eight digits which represents the number of cents in the entered amount.

```
PROCEDURE GETBUCK(VAR BUCK:BUCKTYPE);
VAR SPOS:INTEGER;
    RSTRING:STOCKNAME;
    PNUM:BUCKTYPE;
BEGIN
 NUMSTRING(RSTRING);
 IF LENGTH(RSTRING)< >0 THEN
   BEGIN
      IF POS('.',RSTRING) = 0 THEN RSTRING: = CONCAT(RSTRING,'.00');
      IF POS('.',RSTRING) = LENGTH(RSTRING) – 1 THEN
        RSTRING: = CONCAT(RSTRING,'0');
      PNUM: = 0;
      FOR SPOS: = 1 TO LENGTH(RSTRING) DO
```

```
        BEGIN
          IF RSTRING[SPOS] < >    '.'   THEN
            BEGIN
              PNUM: = PNUM*  10 + ORD(RSTRING[SPOS]) – ORD('0');
            END;
        END;   (*FOR SPOS*)
      BUCK: = PNUM;
    END;
END;
```

The GETINTEGER procedure allows the entry of a positive integer with a maximum value of 32767. The procedure actually calls GETREAL to get a real number, then truncates the result to an integer.

```
PROCEDURE GETINTEGER(VAR INUM:INTEGER);
VAR   RNUM:REAL;
BEGIN
  RNUM: = INUM/1;
  GETREAL(RNUM);
  IF RNUM > 32767.0 THEN RNUM: = 32767.0;
  INUM: = TRUNC(RNUM);
END;   (*GETINTEGER*)
```

Printing a Right-Justified String

The FILLWRITE procedure is used to display a string with right-justification in a field of specified length. It is useful when lining up columns of data on the screen. The maximum length of the string which will be properly displayed is 25 characters—this is set by the length of the fill constant. Twenty-five characters happens to be the length of the longest string data type in the program from which this procedure was excerpted. To display a longer string, increase the length of the fill constant.

```
PROCEDURE FILLWRITE(INSTRING:STRING; LENGTH:INTEGER);
CONST FILL = '                 ';
VAR   TSTRING:STRING;
BEGIN
  TSTRING: = CONCAT(INSTRING,FILL);
  TSTRING: = COPY(TSTRING,1,LENGTH);
  WRITE(TSTRING);
END;
```

Disk Input and Output

The following procedure, IOPRINT, is called when a disk I/O error occurs. The procedure is called with an integer parameter which defines what type of error has occurred. This number may be the IORESULT value returned when an I/O operation is carried out with system error checking disabled with the (*$I – *) option in effect.

```
PROCEDURE   IOPRINT(ERRTYPE:INTEGER);
BEGIN
  GOTOXY(0,22);
  WRITE(CHR(7));
  CASE ERRTYPE OF
      1:WRITELN('DISK READ ERROR.');
      2:WRITELN('BAD UNIT NUMBER.');
      3:WRITELN('ILLEGAL OPERATION.');
      4:WRITELN('UNDEFINED HARDWARE ERROR.');
      5:WRITELN('UNIT NO LONGER ON LINE.');
      6:WRITELN('FILE NOT IN DIRECTORY.');
      7:WRITELN('ILLEGAL FILE NAME.');
      8:WRITELN('INSUFFICIENT DISK SPACE.');
      9:WRITELN('NO SUCH VOLUME ON LINE.');
     10:WRITELN('NO SUCH FILE IN VOLUME.');
     11:WRITELN('DUPLICATE FILE.');
     12:WRITELN('ATTEMPT TO OPEN AN OPEN FILE.');
     13:WRITELN('FILE NOT OPEN.');
     14:WRITELN('ERROR IN READING INTEGER OR REAL DATA.');
     15:WRITELN('RING BUFFER OVERFLOW.');
  END; (*CASE ERRTYPE*)
END; (*IOPRINT*)
```

The NODISK procedure notifies the user if a required diskette is not available in one of the disk drives. If a required disk is not on line, an error message is displayed on line 22 and the routine waits for a key to be pressed before returning to the calling procedure. If some other type of disk error has occurred, the IOPRINT routine is called. This procedure is generally called by another procedure which opens a file (see OPENCLIENT below).

```
PROCEDURE NODISK(DISKNAME:STRING;
                 DISKERR:INTEGER);
VAR CH:CHAR;
BEGIN
    IF (DISKERR<>0)AND(DISKERR<>9) THEN IOPRINT(DISKERR);
    IF(DISKERR=9) THEN
      BEGIN
        GOTOXY(0,22);
        WRITELN('NO  ', DISKNAME,'  DISKETTE!');
        WRITELN('PLEASE INSERT DISKETTE AND HIT ANY KEY');
        READ(KEYBOARD,CH);
      END;
END;  (*DISKERR*)
```

The OPENCLIENT procedure opens a file on a particular diskette. The file to be opened is a globally-declared data file. System error checking is disabled, and the NODISK procedure is called. If an error other than number 9—No such volume on line—occurs, the program will be unable to recover. Fatal errors of this type usually occur when a diskette is damaged or there is a hardware problem with the computer. When these errors occur the user must hit the reset key and call the programmer.

```
PROCEDURE  OPENCLIENT;
VAR IOERR:INTEGER;
BEGIN
  REPEAT
    (*$I-*)
    RESET(CLFILE,'NCLIENT:CLIENTS.DATA');
    (*$I+*)
    IOERR:=IORESULT;
    NODISK('CLIENTS',IOERR);
  UNTIL IOERR=0;
END;  (*OPENCLIENT*)
```

Appendix II

The Programmer's Cross Reference

This appendix is an alphabetized listing of the most often used keywords in BASIC. Opposite each BASIC keyword is its equivalent in Pascal. Thus, if you try to write a Pascal program, but have trouble deciding how to construct a program segment which would be simple in BASIC, this appendix should help you.

Algebraic Operators

	BASIC		PASCAL
=	Assign value to variable	:=	Assign value to variable
−	Negation (with single variable)	−	Negation (with single variable)
∧	Exponentiation	EXP(x)	Exponentiation (may require a special unit in UCSD Pascal)
+	Addition	+	Addition
−	Subtraction	−	Subtraction

BASIC	PASCAL
* Multiplication	* Multiplication
/ Division (real and integer)	/ Division (real only)
	DIV Division (integer only)
	MOD Modulus (A MOD B yields the remainder in the division of A by B)
DEF FNX(A) Define function X with real result and real parameter A	Function X(A:real):real; Pascal functions may also have integer, character and sub-range results.
END Halt program with no	END; End of complex statement
Message	END. End of main program
FOR I = 1 TO 100	FOR I: = 1 to 100 DO
(execute some statements)	Begin
NEXT I	(*execute some statements*)
	End;
FOR I = 1 TO 100 STEP 5	No equivalent—Pascal always steps by one.
FRE(0) Returns amount of free memory available to user	MEMAVAIL
GOSUB 100 Execute subroutine at line 100	SUB100 subroutines (procedures or functions) are called by simply referencing their name.
GOTO 100 Unconditional jump line 100	GOTO 100 Unconditional jump to label 100—the use of GOTO is strongly discouraged.

Array definition:

BASIC	PASCAL
DIM A(50), B$(10)	Var A:Array[0 . . 50] of Real; B:Array[0. . 10] of String;

Remember that the default maximum length of a single string in a Pascal array is 80 characters. In most BASICs the default is 255 characters. Also remember that different versions of BASIC have different types of string arrays. See the discussion of S1 and S2 BASICS in chapter 2.

Miscellaneous Functions

BASIC	PASCAL
ASC(A$) Returns ASCII code for first character of string	ORD(Astring[1])
CALL 768 Execute machine-language at address 768	No special command in Pascal. Procedures and functions may be written in machine language—a subject beyond the scope of this book.
CHR$(C) Returns character with ASCII code C	CHR(C) (C must be an integer)
CLEAR Reset all variables to zero	No equivalent in Pascal—you must initialize each variable before use
CONT Continue program halted by STOP, END or Control-C	No equivalent in Pascal unless your system has a Debugger
DATA A,"bstring",C	No equivalent in Pascal
INPUT X,Y$	READLN(X,YSTRING)
INPUT "Enter X: ";X	No equivalent in Pascal—you must use two statements:

```
    WRITE('Enter X: ');
    READLN(X);
```

Loop Structures.   Pascal has two loop structures (in addition to the FOR loop), which allow you to test the terminating condition either before or after the statements inside the loop are executed.

Test Before Execution.   In this example, data are read into an array until the desired number of points are entered. Entering a number of points which is zero or negative results in no data being entered. The test must be done before the array element is defined or it would be possible to cause an error by trying to store data in the −1 element of the array.

BASIC	PASCAL
100 INPUT "NUMBER OF POINTS? ";NP	Write('Number of points? ');
110 P = 1	Readln(Numpoint);
120 IF P>NP THEN GOTO 200	PNUM: = 1;
130 PRINT "POINT VALUE ";	While Pnum < = Numpoint Do
140 INPUT PT(P)	Begin
150 P = P + 1	Write('Point Value? ');
160 GOTO 120	Readln(Point[Pnum]);
200 REM EXIT LOOP HERE	Pnum: = Pnum + 1;
	End;

Test After Execution. In this example, data is entered until an End-of-Data value is entered. The End-of-Data mark (a -1 value) is saved in the array for later use.

BASIC	PASCAL
100 PRINT "ENTER -1 AS LAST ITEM"	Writeln('Enter -1 as last item');
110 PN = 1	Pnum: = 1;
120 PRINT "POINT #"; PN;" VALUE"	Repeat
130 INPUT PT(PN)	Writeln('Point #',Pnum,'Value?');
140 PN = PN + 1	Readln(Point[Pnum]);
150 IF PT(PN − 1) < > − 1 THEN GOTO 120	Pnum: = Pnum + 1;
160 REM FALL THROUGH LOOP HERE	Until Point [Pnum − 1] = − 1;

Note that since the array index (PN or Pnum) is incremented before the test, you have to subtract one from it to test the last point value.

Mathematical Functions. Most of the functions in BASIC have equivalents in Pascal. The standard functions are listed here with some notes where there are differences in the two languages. Some versions of Pascal may require a special unit from the system library (TRANSCEND on the Apple) if you want to call some of these functions.

BASIC	PASCAL
ABS	ABS
ATAN	ATAN (in UCSD Pascal)
	ARCTAN (in Standard Pascal)
COS	COS
SIN	SIN
TAN	Not available—use
	SIN(X)/COS(X)
EXP	EXP
LOG natural logarithm	LN
	LOG logarithm base 10
SQR(X) Square root of X	SQRT(X)
	SQR Returns X squared
INT	TRUNC Returns integer part of real
	ROUND Rounds a real number to the nearest integer
RND(1) Returns a random number from 0 to 0.999999	RANDOM Returns a random integer from 0 to 32767
	RANDOMIZE Set a new seed value for the random number generator
SGN(X) Returns -1 if $X < 0$, 0 if $X = 0$ and 1 if $X > 0$	No equivalent in Pascal, but the function can easily be written.

INDEX

Arrays, Manipulation as unit   34
Arrays, in Pascal and BASIC   33
BASIC, differences in I/O   4
BASIC, variations in strings in   3
BLOCKREAD function   47
BLOCKWRITE function   47
Boolean Variables   16
Byte, as simplest data structure   13
CASE statements   68
CHAR variables   16
CLOSE statement   41
CLOSE statement, options with   41
Commas, as number separators   57
Compiler options   86
Compiler program   85
Console input   51
DATSTRING procedure   103
DELAY procedure   101
DOWNTO, used with FOR
   loop   63
Data files, WARNING NOTE   36
Data files, creation of   37
Declarations section, introduc-
   tion   6
Device numbers, for APPLE II   49
Dynamic variables   95
EOF statement   44
Editor, text manipulation pro-
   gram   84
Explicit numeric formatting   53
FILLWRITE procedure   109
FOR loops, introduction   62
Field width designator   53
Filer, file manipulation program   82
GET statement   41
GETBUCK procedure   108
GETCHAR function   101
GETDATE procedure   104
GETINTEGER procedure   108
GETREAL procedure   107
GETSTRING procedure   102

GOTO statement   70
GOTOXY procedure   55
Global variables   78
Graphics, in UCSD system   92
IF statements   67
IOPRINT procedure   110
Integer data type   14
KEYPRESS function   100
Library files   97
Linker program   87
Local variables   79
NODISK procedure   111
NUMSTRING procedure   106
Nesting of procedures and func-
tions   76
OPENCLIENT procedure   111
PAGE procedure   55
PRINT USING vs. Field width   54
PUT statement   40
Packed Arrays   35
Packed Records   31
Packed records, WARNING NOTE
   32
Pascal, origins of language   2
Pointers   96
Printer, as output device   59
Printers, opening and closing   59
Program blocks, introduction   8
Program name statement   6
Prompts, with console input   51
READLN procedure   56
READLN statement   48
REPEAT. . .UNTIL loops   64
RESET statement   41
REWRITE statement   38
Real numbers, as data type   15
Record Data type, definition   28
Rule of Closing   40
Rule of READLN   57
SEEK statement   42
STRING variables   17

Scalar variables   20
Scalars, SUCC and PRED func-
      tions   21
Sets as data types   25
Sets, limitations of UCSD
      Pascal   25
Sets, operations on 26
Strings, apostrophe as delimiter   55
Structured language, definition
      of   5
Subrange variables   23
Swapping mode option   87
TAB command, lacking in
      Pascal   56
Text files   47
Top-down programming   74
UNITCLEAR procedure   50

UNITREAD procedure   49
UNITWRITE procedure   49
Units, as program segments   88
Untyped Data Files   45
User libraries   97
Utility programs for UCSD
      Pascal   90
Variant records   94
Video screen formatting   55
WHILE. . .DO loops   66
WITH statement   29
WRITE statement, as input
      prompt   52
WRITEBUCKS procedure   106
Writer's Rule, for output for-
      mat   53
Window variable   39